AI Wealth Igniter

Master the Intelligence Explosion to Trade Profitably, Invest Smarter, and Build Unbreakable Wealth

Ryan Harper

RIVANNA HEIGHTS MEDIA

Rivanna Heights Media

Also by Rivanna Heights Media

Don't Get Over It by Sophia Wells
The 60-Day AI Advantage by Ryan Harper
Epic Historical Mysteries by Logan Cross
AI-Proof Your Career by Ryan Harper
Conspiracy Theories Unveiled by Logan Cross
Pickleball Made Simple by Blake Foster
The Complete Beginner's Guide To ChatGPT by Ryan Harper
Cryptocurrency Investing 101 by Jordan Taylor

Contents

Join the Day Trading Masterclass Waitlist!

As a thank you for purchasing this book, you're invited to join the waitlist for an exclusive Day Trading Masterclass.

In this exclusive masterclass, I teach the exact technical strategy I use to trade the markets — a precise, repeatable system built for traders who want consistent, real-world results.

Inside the masterclass:

- A full breakdown of my trading strategy
- Chart setups, entry/exit rules, and trade management techniques
- How to develop a disciplined trader’s mindset

Why join the waitlist?

Seats are limited, and demand is high. The waitlist gives you **priority access** as spots open — first come, first served.

Secure your spot on the waitlist now by clicking or scanning the QR code below:

The Intelligence Explosion Fortune Window

The next few years will create more millionaires than any period in modern history.

This isn't hyperbole or another get-rich-quick promise. It's a mathematical certainty driven by the greatest technological shift since the internet's birth. Artificial intelligence isn't just changing how we work—it's rewriting the rules of wealth creation itself. The intelligence explosion has begun, and those who position themselves correctly will capture gains that seemed impossible just years ago.

The window is closing faster than you think.

The Wealth-Building Crisis You're Facing

Right now, you're caught in an impossible situation. You've built your success through careful planning, strategic thinking, and calculated risks. You've accumulated significant capital—anywhere from $50,000 to $50 million or more. You understand markets, you know business, and you've created wealth before.

But AI has changed everything.

Every day, you watch headlines about AI breakthroughs that could make entire industries obsolete overnight. You see companies valued at billions based on AI potential alone. You witness your competitors talking about AI strategies while you're still trying to figure out if this is the real deal or just another bubble.

The fear keeps you awake at night. What if you miss this opportunity? What if you invest wrong and lose everything you've built? What if AI makes your current business model irrelevant? What if you become one of those cautionary tales—successful people who got left behind by technological change?

You're not alone in this struggle. Across the country, successful entrepreneurs and investors are grappling with the same three core challenges:

1. **Timing Anxiety**: When is the right moment to make your move? Too early, and you're gambling on hype. Too late, and you've missed the wealth-creation window.

2. **Strategy Confusion**: Should you invest in AI companies, start an AI business, or find another approach entirely? The options seem endless, but most carry enormous risk.

3. **Relevance Fear**: How do you ensure your wealth and influence survive when AI potentially disrupts everything you know?

The conventional wisdom is failing you.

Traditional investment advice tells you to "diversify and hold." But diversification won't help when entire sectors get disrupted simultaneously. The "buy and hold" strategy assumes gradual change, not the exponential transformation AI brings.

Financial advisors recommend "safe" investments like bonds and blue-chip stocks. But safe investments won't generate the returns needed to keep pace with AI-driven market explosions. Playing it safe during the intelligence explosion is actually the riskiest strategy of all.

Even AI investment experts focus on picking individual AI stocks or funding AI startups. But this approach requires deep technical knowledge you don't have, and the failure rate is catastrophic. Most AI companies will fail, and even experts struggle to predict which ones will succeed.

You need a different approach entirely.

The Intelligence Explosion Advantage

Here's what most people don't understand about the intelligence explosion: the biggest wealth won't come from building AI companies or picking AI stocks. It'll come from positioning yourself to capture the broad market surges that AI adoption creates.

Think about it logically. When AI increases productivity across entire industries, stock markets rise. When AI reduces costs for major corporations, their profits soar. When AI creates new consumer behaviors, multiple sectors benefit simultaneously. The intelligence explosion lifts all boats—if you're positioned correctly.

This is your competitive advantage.

While others chase individual AI companies, you'll capture the entire market's AI-driven growth. While others try to predict which AI technologies will win, you'll profit from the overall technological advancement. While others risk everything on specific bets, you'll use proven financial instruments to extract wealth with controlled risk.

The FIRE Framework gives you this advantage. Instead of gambling on AI companies, you'll use systematic market timing to capture broad-based gains. Instead of trying to predict the future, you'll profit from the present reality of AI-driven market movements. Instead of risking everything on speculation, you'll build wealth through disciplined financial strategies.

Let me show you how this works.

The FIRE Framework Foundation

The AI Wealth Igniter operates on a simple principle: extract gains from market volatility, then use those gains to build permanent wealth structures. This isn't about getting rich quick—it's about getting rich systematically.

The framework has four distinct phases:

Focus involves identifying optimal market entry points during AI-driven volatility. You'll learn to recognize when and in which direction broad market indexes are trending. Using technical analysis and economic indicators, you'll time your entries for maximum upside potential.

Invest means deploying specific financial instruments to capture these market movements. You'll use index futures, options, and leveraged ETFs to amplify your gains while controlling your risk. This strategic use of proven financial tools limits exposure and defines downside risk.

Reinvest transforms your market gains into scalable business ownership. You'll identify and acquire businesses with strong fundamentals that will thrive in an AI-dominated economy. This shifts your wealth from public markets to private business ownership.

Endure creates permanent wealth structures that survive any economic change. You'll diversify your business portfolio, establish legal protection structures, and build systems that generate wealth regardless of AI's future development.

Each phase builds on the previous one.

The Focus phase typically takes 2-3 months to master. You'll develop the skills to identify market opportunities and time your entries effectively. Most people never move beyond this phase because they become addicted to trading gains. But trading gains are temporary—business ownership is permanent.

The Invest phase runs concurrently with Focus. You'll deploy your capital using leveraged instruments to capture 3-5x the returns of standard market investing. The key is using defined-risk strategies that limit your downside while maximizing your upside.

The Reinvest phase begins once you've generated significant trading profits. You'll use these gains to acquire businesses with proven models, predictable cash flows, and scalability potential. This is where temporary gains become permanent wealth.

The Endure phase ensures your wealth survives any future changes. You'll build diversified business portfolios, legal structures, and systems that generate wealth independently of any single economic trend or technological development.

The timeline is critical.

Why the First Few Years Are Critical

The intelligence explosion follows predictable patterns. New technologies create initial uncertainty, which creates market volatility. Smart money recognizes the opportunity and begins positioning. Early adopters capture the majority of gains before mainstream adoption stabilizes markets.

We're currently in the volatility phase. AI adoption is accelerating, but markets haven't fully priced in the implications. This creates the perfect conditions for systematic wealth extraction using the FIRE Framework.

Historical precedent supports this timeline.

During the internet boom of the late 1990s, the major wealth-creation window lasted approximately 24 months. Those who positioned themselves correctly during 1998-2000 captured gains that sustained them through the subsequent crash and beyond.

The mobile revolution of 2007-2009 followed similar patterns. Apple's iPhone launch created market opportunities that extended far beyond Apple stock. Companies positioned to benefit from mobile adoption saw massive gains, while those who missed the window struggled to catch up.

The current AI explosion shows identical characteristics. Market volatility driven by AI uncertainty creates opportunities for systematic wealth extraction. Companies adapting to AI see valuations multiply. Entire sectors experience boom-bust cycles based on AI adoption timelines.

The difference now is speed.

AI development and adoption happen faster than previous technological revolutions. What took years during the internet boom now happens in months. The intelligence explosion's wealth-creation window is shorter but more intense than anything we've seen before.

This means you must act decisively. The systematic approach of the FIRE Framework gives you the tools to capture these opportunities without excessive risk. But the window won't stay open indefinitely.

Your Transformation Journey

Over the next 36 months, you'll undergo a fundamental transformation. You'll evolve from someone anxious about AI's impact to someone who systematically profits from it. You'll shift from fearing disruption to creating wealth from volatility.

Months 1-3: Foundation Building

You'll master the Focus phase, learning to identify market opportunities using technical analysis and economic indicators. You'll develop the discipline to wait for optimal entry points rather than chasing every market movement. Using trade simulation initially allows you to refine and test your strategies.

Months 4-36 (or longer): Wealth Extraction

You'll deploy the Invest phase, using leveraged instruments to capture market trends and surges. You'll experience the satisfaction of systematic gains that compound your wealth without gambling your future.

Months 10 and on: Business Acquisition

You'll implement the Reinvest phase, using your market gains to acquire scalable businesses that are well-positioned for predictable cash flows. You'll transition from market timing to business ownership, creating permanent wealth structures.

Months 19 and on: Wealth Preservation

You'll enter the Endure phase, building diversified portfolios of companies and legal structures that protect your wealth. You'll establish systems that generate returns regardless of market conditions.

The transformation is measurable, and your results will depend on your commitment to the system.

The Difference This Makes

Imagine checking your portfolio in 18 months and seeing gains that seemed impossible today. Imagine owning businesses that generate cash flow regardless of market conditions. Imagine having the financial security to pursue opportunities instead of worrying about disruption.

This isn't fantasy—it's the predictable result of systematic wealth extraction during technological explosions. The intelligence explosion creates opportunities, and the FIRE Framework gives you the tools to capture them.

You'll gain three critical advantages:

1. **Market Timing Mastery**: You'll develop the skills to identify and act on op-

timal market opportunities in trending and volatile markets. This skill compounds your wealth regardless of future technological developments.

2. **Business Portfolio Ownership**: You'll build a diversified collection of businesses positioned to thrive in an AI-dominated economy. This creates wealth that survives any single market cycle or technological change.

3. **Strategic Wealth Preservation**: You'll understand and establish legal structures and systems that protect your wealth from future uncertainties. This ensures your gains compound rather than disappear during market downturns.

Most importantly, you'll gain control.

Instead of fearing AI's impact on the business environment, you'll profit from it. Instead of wondering if you're missing opportunities, you'll systematically capture them. Instead of worrying about future disruption, you'll build wealth structures that thrive on change.

The Choice Before You

You have two paths forward. You can continue struggling with AI anxiety, paralyzed by fear of making the wrong decision. You can keep watching opportunities pass while you debate whether this is the right time to act.

Or you can embrace the systematic approach that transforms uncertainty into wealth.

The intelligence explosion isn't waiting for you to feel ready.

Every day you delay is a day of potential gains lost forever. The market volatility that creates opportunities today will stabilize as AI adoption becomes mainstream. The business acquisition targets available now will become more expensive as their AI advantages become obvious.

The wealth-creation window is open, but it's closing. The question isn't whether you should act—it's whether you'll act systematically or continue paralyzed by uncertainty.

This is your moment.

The FIRE Framework gives you the tools to capture wealth from the intelligence explosion while others remain frozen by fear. You have the capital, the experience, and the strategic thinking necessary to implement this system successfully.

The next few years will determine your entire financial future. You can spend them worrying about AI's impact, or you can spend them systematically building wealth from AI's opportunities.

The choice is yours, but the window won't wait.

Now that you understand the magnitude of the opportunity and the systematic approach to capture it, you're ready to learn the specific skills that separate successful AI-era investors from those who get left behind. The first step is recognizing authentic market signals that indicate real opportunity rather than speculative hype—a skill that will serve as your foundation for everything that follows.

Part I: Decode

Rivanna Heights Media

Chapter One

The Intelligence Explosion

Fortune favors those who recognize signals before they become obvious.

Most investors today stand paralyzed at the crossroads of the greatest wealth creation opportunity in human history. They're drowning in contradictory information, unable to separate authentic market signals from the endless stream of AI hype flooding their feeds. Meanwhile, the small group of informed investors who can decode these signals are positioning themselves to capture exponential gains that will define generational wealth.

The intelligence explosion is here, and it's creating the most concentrated wealth transfer window we've seen since the early days of the internet.

The Hidden Pattern Behind Every Technology Revolution

History teaches us that massive wealth transfers follow predictable patterns. The railroad boom of the 1840s, the oil rush of the early 1900s, the internet explosion of the 1990s—each followed the same fundamental structure. An emerging technology reaches a tipping point, early adopters position themselves strategically, and within a narrow window, extraordinary wealth concentrates among those who recognized the signals first.

The intelligence explosion follows this exact pattern, but with one crucial difference: **the speed of transformation is accelerating at an unprecedented rate**. What took the internet 20+ years to accomplish, AI is achieving at an alarming rate. This compression creates both the greatest opportunity and the greatest risk of our lifetime.

Consider the internet's wealth creation timeline. In 1995, most people didn't understand what the web meant for business. By 1999, early internet investors had captured gains that seemed impossible just four years earlier. Amazon's stock price increased 2,300% between 1997 and 1999. Those who recognized the authentic signals and positioned themselves correctly during this narrow window built fortunes that lasted decades.

The intelligence explosion is following the same pattern, but the window is narrower and the gains are potentially much larger. **The question isn't whether AI will create massive wealth—it's whether you'll position yourself to capture it.**

Separating Signal from Noise in the AI Revolution

The biggest challenge facing investors today isn't finding information about AI—it's filtering through the overwhelming amount of contradictory data to identify what actually matters. Every day brings new headlines about AI breakthroughs, market predictions, and investment opportunities. Most of this information is either speculative noise or marketing designed to separate you from your money.

Real wealth builders focus on three categories of authentic signals that predict genuine market movement:

1. Infrastructure Investment Patterns

The most reliable predictor of technology adoption isn't what companies say they're going to do—it's what they're actually spending money on. When you see consistent, large-scale infrastructure investments across multiple sectors, you're witnessing the foundation being laid for explosive growth.

Current infrastructure signals include:

- **Data center construction**: Global data center capacity is expanding by 35% annually, with major tech companies investing over $200 billion in new facilities specifically designed for AI workloads
- **Semiconductor manufacturing**: TSMC, Intel, and other chip manufacturers are investing over $400 billion in new fabrication facilities to meet AI chip demand
- **Network infrastructure**: 5G deployment and fiber optic expansion are accelerating to support AI applications requiring massive bandwidth

- **Cloud computing capacity**: Amazon, Microsoft, and Google are expanding their cloud infrastructure at unprecedented rates to support AI services

These investments represent committed capital that companies must recoup through revenue growth. When you see this level of infrastructure spending, you're looking at a market that's preparing for massive demand increases.

2. Regulatory and Policy Shifts

Government actions often predict market movements months or years before they become obvious to individual investors. Policy changes create both opportunities and constraints that smart investors can anticipate.

Key regulatory signals include:

- **AI safety regulations**: New frameworks for AI governance create barriers to entry that benefit established players
- **Data privacy laws**: Regulations like GDPR and emerging AI-specific laws create compliance costs that favor larger companies
- **Trade policies**: Export controls on AI technology and semiconductors reshape global supply chains
- **Government AI initiatives**: National AI strategies and funding programs signal where public investment will flow

Understanding these regulatory trends helps you position your investments ahead of market-moving policy announcements.

3. Cross-Industry Adoption Metrics

The most powerful signal comes from tracking AI adoption across industries that aren't traditionally associated with technology. When conservative sectors like insurance, agriculture, and manufacturing begin implementing AI solutions at scale, you're witnessing the beginning of a broader economic transformation.

Current adoption signals include:

- **Healthcare**: AI diagnostic tools are being deployed in over 60% of major hospital systems

- **Financial services**: Banks are implementing AI for fraud detection, risk assessment, and customer service
- **Manufacturing**: Predictive maintenance and quality control AI systems are being adopted across automotive, aerospace, and industrial sectors
- **Retail**: Inventory management, demand forecasting, and personalization AI tools are becoming standard

This cross-industry adoption creates a multiplier effect. As AI proves its value in one sector, adjacent industries accelerate their adoption, creating a self-reinforcing cycle of growth.

The Critical Wealth Window

The intelligence explosion creates a unique timing dynamic that differs from previous technology revolutions. While the internet's wealth creation window extended over roughly a decade, AI's impact is compressed into a much shorter timeframe.

This compression occurs because:

AI builds on existing infrastructure: Unlike the internet, which required building entirely new infrastructure, AI leverages existing computing, networking, and data systems. This allows for faster deployment and adoption.

Network effects accelerate: Each AI implementation makes the next one easier and more valuable. This creates exponential rather than linear growth curves.

Capital availability is unprecedented: Unlike previous technology revolutions, AI development has access to massive amounts of capital from the beginning. This eliminates many of the funding constraints that slowed earlier technology adoption.

The result is a **several-year window where the greatest wealth creation opportunities exist**. This window started in late 2022 with the release of ChatGPT and will likely close by early 2030 as AI adoption and integration becomes standard across most industries.

Understanding this timeline is crucial for strategic positioning. The investors who build substantial wealth from the intelligence explosion will be those who recognize we're currently in the early phase of this window and position themselves accordingly.

Identifying Market Explosion Signals

Market explosion signals are specific, measurable indicators that predict when AI-driven growth will accelerate beyond current expectations. These signals allow you to position your investments before the broader market recognizes the opportunity.

Technical Adoption Signals

Monitor these specific metrics to identify when AI adoption is reaching critical mass:

- **API usage growth**: Track usage statistics for major AI platforms like OpenAI, Anthropic, and Google's AI services
- **Developer activity**: Monitor GitHub repositories, Stack Overflow discussions, and developer conference attendance related to AI
- **Enterprise software integration**: Track how quickly major enterprise software companies are integrating AI features
- **Patent filings**: Follow AI-related patent applications as an indicator of corporate investment in AI technology

Economic Signals

These financial indicators predict when AI impact will translate into market movement:

- **Productivity metrics**: Track productivity improvements in early AI-adopting industries
- **Cost reduction data**: Monitor how AI implementation affects operational costs across different sectors
- **Revenue growth patterns**: Analyze companies reporting AI-driven revenue increases
- **Investment flows**: Track venture capital and private equity investment in AI companies

Market Structure Signals

These broader market indicators suggest when AI will drive significant price movements:

- **Sector rotation**: Watch for investment flows shifting toward AI-beneficiary sectors

- **Valuation premiums**: Monitor how the market values companies with AI integration versus those without
- **Merger and acquisition activity**: Track M&A deals where AI capabilities are the primary value driver
- **IPO market activity**: Follow public offerings of AI companies as an indicator of market appetite

Building Your Signal Recognition Framework

To capitalize on the intelligence explosion, you need a systematic approach to signal recognition. This framework ensures you're making decisions based on data rather than emotions or speculation.

Step 1: Establish Your Information Sources

Create a curated list of reliable information sources that provide authentic signals rather than speculation:

- **Financial data providers**: Bloomberg, Reuters, and other professional-grade financial information services
- **Industry research**: Reports from Gartner, McKinsey, and other consulting firms with track records of accurate technology predictions
- **Government data**: Economic statistics, regulatory filings, and policy documents that provide objective metrics
- **Corporate communications**: Earnings calls, investor presentations, and SEC filings from major technology companies

Step 2: Create Your Signal Dashboard

Develop a systematic way to track the signals that matter most:

- **Infrastructure metrics**: Track data center capacity, semiconductor production, and network expansion
- **Adoption metrics**: Monitor cross-industry AI implementation and usage sta-

tistics

- **Financial metrics**: Follow investment flows, revenue growth, and productivity improvements
- **Market metrics**: Track sector performance, valuation trends, and trading volumes

Step 3: Establish Decision Criteria

Define specific thresholds that trigger your investment decisions:

- **Signal strength**: Determine how many positive signals you need before taking action
- **Signal duration**: Establish minimum time periods for signal persistence before acting
- **Signal correlation**: Require signals from multiple categories to confirm trends
- **Signal contradiction**: Create rules for handling conflicting signals

Avoid the Speculation Trap

The biggest risk facing investors today isn't missing the intelligence explosion—it's getting caught in speculation masquerading as investment opportunity. The AI boom has created countless opportunities for uninformed investors to lose money quickly.

Common Speculation Traps

Avoid these common mistakes that destroy wealth instead of building it:

- **Chasing AI stock prices**: Buying stocks simply because they're associated with AI without understanding the underlying business fundamentals
- **Following social media hype**: Making investment decisions based on information from unverified sources on social media platforms
- **Timing short-term volatility**: Trying to profit from daily or weekly stock price movements without a longer-term strategy
- **Investing in unproven technologies**: Putting money into AI applications that

haven't demonstrated real-world value

The Fundamentals-First Approach
Instead of speculating, focus on companies and opportunities with strong fundamental characteristics:

- **Proven business models**: Invest in companies that are using AI to improve existing profitable operations
- **Competitive advantages**: Look for businesses where AI creates sustainable competitive moats
- **Scalable economics**: Focus on opportunities where AI improves unit economics and profit margins
- **Market positioning**: Invest in companies that are leaders in their industries with the resources to implement AI effectively

Your Signal Recognition Action Plan
To implement everything you've learned in this chapter, follow this systematic action plan:

Week 1-2: Information Infrastructure
Set up your information sources and signal dashboard
Establish daily routines for monitoring key metrics
Create a system for documenting and tracking signals

Week 3-4: Market Analysis
Apply your signal recognition framework to current market conditions
Identify which signals are currently strongest
Assess the current phase of the intelligence explosion timeline

Week 5-6: Strategy Development
Use your signal analysis to identify specific investment opportunities
Develop position sizing and risk management rules
Create decision criteria for when to act on signals

Week 7-8: Implementation Preparation

Prepare your investment accounts and tools

Establish your initial positions based on signal strength

Set up monitoring systems for ongoing signal tracking

The Foundation for Strategic Wealth Building

The intelligence explosion signal recognition skills you've developed in this chapter form the foundation for everything that follows. Without the ability to distinguish authentic opportunities from speculation, even the most sophisticated investment strategies will fail. You will build your technical analysis and market timing decisions around the overall AI landscape, knowing that this key determinant is what will drive trends in the market.

The infrastructure investments, regulatory changes, and cross-industry adoption patterns you've learned to recognize are creating the conditions for exponential market growth. More importantly, you have the framework to continue identifying these foundational signals as they evolve.

Your next step is to honestly assess your current capacity for implementing leveraged market strategies during this period of opportunity. The intelligence explosion creates unprecedented wealth-building potential, but only for those who can accurately evaluate their financial foundation and risk tolerance. In the next chapter, we'll examine how to perform this crucial self-assessment and ensure you're positioned to capitalize on the opportunities you're now equipped to recognize.

Chapter Two

Your Market Trading Foundation

Most investors fail because they never honestly assess their true capacity. Warren Buffett once said, "Risk comes from not knowing what you're doing," and this wisdom becomes even more critical during the intelligence explosion. Many ambitious entrepreneurs believe their business success automatically translates to market trading prowess, but this assumption has destroyed more wealth than any market crash ever could. The difference between those who build unbreakable wealth and those who watch opportunities slip away lies in one fundamental truth: brutal self-honesty about your trading foundation.

Before you can harness the explosive potential of investment markets, you must first understand your own financial and emotional infrastructure. This chapter isn't about market analysis or trading strategies—it's about you. Your capital capacity, your risk tolerance, and your emotional resilience will determine whether you emerge from the intelligence explosion with generational wealth or painful lessons about overconfidence.

The investors who thrive during this historic opportunity share one common trait: they know exactly where they stand before they make their first move. They've measured their true capacity, not their wishful thinking. They've stress-tested their emotional responses, not just their spreadsheets. And they've built their wealth extraction strategy on rock-solid foundations, not on hopes and assumptions.

The Capital Allocation Reality Check

Your first step toward AI wealth mastery requires an unflinching look at your actual capital position. This isn't about how much money you have—it's about how much you can realistically deploy in leveraged market strategies without jeopardizing your core financial security.

Here's what separates successful AI-era investors from those who get swept away by market turbulence: they never confuse their total net worth with their tradeable capital. Your business equity, your primary residence, your emergency fund, and your retirement accounts aren't part of your trading foundation. They're the bedrock that supports your wealth-building activities, not the fuel that powers them.

The Three-Tier Capital Assessment Framework

Your capital allocation strategy must follow a disciplined three-tier approach that protects your downside while maximizing your upside potential during the intelligence explosion.

Tier 1: Survival Capital (50-70% of liquid assets)

This is your financial fortress—the money that ensures you can weather any storm. Your survival capital includes 3-12 months of living expenses, business operating capital, and emergency reserves. This money never touches leveraged positions, never chases market opportunities, and never gets deployed during even the most compelling market dips.

Think of survival capital as your financial oxygen. You can't build wealth if you can't breathe. During the dot-com crash of 2000-2002, investors who maintained substantial survival capital could hold their positions through the downturn and capitalize on the recovery. Those who didn't were forced to sell at the worst possible moments.

Tier 2: Growth Capital (20-35% of liquid assets)

This is your wealth-building engine—the money specifically allocated for market opportunities and business investments. Growth capital participates in your FIRE Framework strategies, funds your leveraged positions, and captures the exponential gains available during the intelligence explosion.

Your growth capital should be money you can afford to lose without changing your lifestyle or compromising your financial security. This is more than a theoretical exercise—you need to genuinely feel comfortable with the possibility of losing every dollar in this tier. If losing your growth capital would force you to downsize your home, pull your kids from private school, or significantly alter your standard of living, you've allocated too much.

Tier 3: Speculation Capital (5-15% of liquid assets)

This is your high-risk, high-reward allocation for the most aggressive opportunities. Speculation capital might fund individual AI stocks, cryptocurrency positions, or other high-volatility investments that could generate returns of 10x or more or complete losses.

Most investors make the fatal mistake of treating all their available capital as speculation capital. They see an opportunity and deploy everything they can access, without considering the psychological and financial pressure this creates. When your entire financial future depends on a single trade or investment, you'll make emotional decisions that destroy your wealth.

Capital Allocation Assessment Table

Capital Tier	Percentage Range	Risk Level	Purpose	Deployment Strategy
Survival	50-70%	Zero	Financial Security	Never deployed in markets
Growth	20-35%	Moderate	Wealth Building	FIRE Framework strategies
Speculation	5-15%	High	Maximum Returns	Aggressive opportunities

Risk Tolerance vs. Risk Capacity

Understanding your risk tolerance is way more than filling out a cookie-cutter questionnaire on your broker's website. It's about honestly assessing how you'll react when your leveraged positions swing 30-40% in a single day—and during the intelligence explosion, these swings will happen regularly.

Your risk tolerance and risk capacity are two completely different things, and confusing them will sabotage your wealth-building efforts. Risk capacity is mathematical—it's how much you can afford to lose based on your financial situation. Risk tolerance is psychological—it's how much volatility you can handle without making destructive emotional decisions.

The Volatility Stress Test

Before you deploy any capital in leveraged instruments, you need to understand how you'll react to significant portfolio swings. The intelligence explosion will create market conditions unlike anything most investors have experienced. AI breakthroughs will trigger massive rallies followed by sharp corrections as markets try to price in rapidly changing fundamentals.

Consider this scenario: You've deployed $5,000 in leveraged positions to capture market gains. In the first week, your positions gain 45%, giving you a $2,250 gain. You're feeling confident and considering increasing your position size. Then, over the next two weeks, a combination of profit-taking and regulatory concerns creates a 35% decline in your positions. Your $7,250 portfolio is now worth $4,700—you're down more than $2,500 from the peak, and lost almost 6% of your original investment.

How do you react? Do you:

- Panic and sell everything to prevent further losses?
- Hold your positions and trust your analysis?
- Add to your positions to take advantage of lower prices?
- Increase your position size because you're convinced the dip is temporary?

Your honest answer to this question reveals your true risk tolerance. If you're not completely comfortable with the possibility of watching significant gains evaporate and potentially losing your entire allocation, you're not ready for leveraged strategies during the intelligence explosion.

Risk Tolerance Indicators

Several factors can help you assess your psychological capacity for handling market volatility:

Sleep Quality: Can you sleep soundly when your positions are down 20-30%? If market movements keep you awake at night, you're overexposed relative to your risk tolerance.

Daily Checking Behavior: Are you checking your positions multiple times per day? Obsessive monitoring usually indicates excessive emotional investment in outcomes.

Relationship Impact: Are market movements affecting your mood, relationships, or daily activities? When trading positions impact your personal life, you've exceeded your psychological capacity.

Decision-Making Clarity: Can you make rational decisions about your positions when they're significantly underwater? Emotional decision-making during drawdowns destroys more wealth than market volatility itself.

Emotional Capacity Assessment

The intelligence explosion will test your emotional resilience in ways that traditional market cycles never could. The combination of massive upside potential and extreme volatility creates a psychological pressure cooker that reveals your true capacity for handling leveraged positions.

The Emotional Roller Coaster Reality

During the intelligence explosion, you'll experience emotional highs and lows that dwarf typical market cycles. One week, you'll feel like a genius as your positions surge 50-60%. The next week, you'll question every decision as the same trading strategy gives back most of its gains. This emotional roller coaster isn't a bug in the system—it's a feature of capturing exponential returns during periods of rapid technological change.

Your emotional capacity determines whether you can ride this roller coaster profitably or get thrown off at the worst possible moments. The investors who build unbreakable wealth during the intelligence explosion share one critical trait: they've prepared themselves emotionally for the journey ahead.

Emotional Capacity Framework

Confidence vs. Arrogance: Confidence allows you to take calculated risks and hold positions through volatility. Arrogance leads you to increase position sizes after wins and ignore warning signals. You need enough confidence to act on opportunities but enough humility to respect market forces.

Patience vs. Impulsiveness: The intelligence explosion will unfold over months and years, not days and weeks. You need the patience to let your positions work while avoiding the impulsive decisions that typically destroy wealth during volatile periods.

Discipline vs. Flexibility: You need the discipline to stick to your predetermined risk management rules while maintaining enough flexibility to adapt to changing market conditions. Rigid adherence to failing strategies destroys wealth, but abandoning proven approaches at the first sign of trouble does the same.

Detachment vs. Engagement: You must care enough about your positions to monitor them properly but remain detached enough to make rational decisions when they move against you. Emotional attachment to specific positions or outcomes clouds your judgment and leads to poor decisions.

Building Your Emotional Foundation

Most investors never develop the emotional capacity for leveraged trading because they jump into the deep end without preparation. You can build your emotional resilience systematically by starting with smaller positions and gradually increasing your exposure as you gain experience and confidence.

Position Sizing Progression: Start with position sizes that allow you to sleep soundly even during maximum anticipated drawdowns. As you gain experience and emotional resilience, you can gradually increase your position sizes while maintaining your psychological comfort level.

Stress Testing: Before deploying significant capital, test your emotional responses with smaller positions. Pay attention to how you feel when positions move against you. Notice your impulses and decision-making patterns under stress.

Mental Rehearsal: Visualize different scenarios and your planned responses. What will you do if your positions drop 30% immediately after entry? How will you handle a 50% gain followed by a 25% decline? Mental rehearsal helps you respond rationally rather than emotionally when these scenarios unfold.

Support Systems: Surround yourself with other serious investors who understand the challenges of leveraged trading. Avoid the echo chambers of social media and online forums that amplify emotional reactions and promote destructive behaviors.

The Foundation Assessment Framework

Your market trading foundation consists of three interconnected components that must all be solid before you can safely deploy leveraged strategies during the intelligence explosion.

<u>Component 1: Financial Capacity</u>

This is your ability to fund leveraged positions without jeopardizing your financial security. It includes your capital allocation strategy, your cash flow situation, and your overall financial stability.

Financial Capacity Checklist:

[ ] You have 3-12 months of living expenses in easily accessible cash

[ ] Your business or career provides stable income independent of your trading activities

[ ] You've allocated specific amounts to survival, growth, and speculation capital
[ ] You can lose your entire growth capital allocation without changing your lifestyle
[ ] You have access to additional capital if exceptional opportunities arise

Component 2: Knowledge Capacity

This is your understanding of leveraged instruments, market dynamics, and the specific opportunities created by the intelligence explosion. Knowledge capacity isn't about predicting market movements—it's about understanding how different instruments behave and how to use them effectively.

Knowledge Capacity Requirements:

[ ] You understand how futures and options work, including their risks and rewards
[ ] You can calculate position sizes based on your risk tolerance and account size
[ ] You understand the relationship between volatility and option pricing
[ ] You know how to use stop-losses and other risk management tools effectively
[ ] You understand the specific dynamics of AI-driven market cycles

Component 3: Psychological Capacity

This is your ability to make rational decisions under pressure and maintain discipline during extreme market conditions. Psychological capacity is often the weakest link in most investors' foundations.

Psychological Capacity Indicators:

[ ] You can hold losing positions without panic selling
[ ] You can take profits without immediately reinvesting everything
[ ] You don't check your positions obsessively throughout the day
[ ] Market movements don't significantly affect your mood or relationships
[ ] You can admit mistakes and adjust your approach when necessary

Foundation Weaknesses That Destroy Wealth

Even successful entrepreneurs often have critical weaknesses in their trading foundation that become apparent only during high-stress market conditions. Identifying and addressing these weaknesses before you deploy leveraged strategies can save you from devastating losses during the intelligence explosion.

The Overconfidence Trap: Business success often creates overconfidence that doesn't translate to market trading. The skills that build successful businesses—taking calculated risks, making quick decisions, and maintaining optimism—can become liabilities in leveraged market strategies.

In business, your decisions directly impact outcomes. You can work harder, improve your product, or adjust your strategy to overcome challenges. In markets, your individual actions have zero impact on price movements. This fundamental difference requires a completely different psychological approach.

The Capital Confusion Problem: Many entrepreneurs confuse their business net worth with their tradeable capital. They see their business equity, real estate holdings, and retirement accounts as available capital for market opportunities. This confusion leads to overextension and forced selling during market downturns.

Your business equity isn't liquid capital—it's an illiquid asset that takes time to convert to cash. Your real estate holdings might be valuable, but they can't be sold quickly without significant costs. Your retirement accounts might be substantial, but accessing them creates tax consequences that destroy your returns.

The Emotional Leverage Amplifier: Leverage amplifies not just your returns but also your emotional reactions. A 10% market move becomes a 30% portfolio move with 3:1 leverage. This amplification creates psychological pressure that most investors aren't prepared to handle.

The emotional impact of leverage isn't linear—it's exponential. A 20% decline in a unleveraged position is disappointing. A 20% decline in a 3:1 leveraged position is a 60% portfolio loss that can trigger panic selling and destroy your wealth-building strategy.

Building Your Personalized Foundation

Your market trading foundation must be specifically designed for your unique situation, goals, and psychological makeup. Cookie-cutter approaches fail because they don't account for individual differences in financial capacity, risk tolerance, and emotional resilience.

The Foundation Blueprint Process

Step 1: Financial Assessment

Calculate your exact capital allocation using the three-tier framework. Be brutally honest about what you can afford to lose without affecting your lifestyle or financial security.

Remember, the goal isn't to maximize your allocation—it's to optimize your allocation for long-term wealth building.

Step 2: Risk Tolerance Calibration
Test your risk tolerance with small positions before deploying significant capital. Start with amounts that feel almost trivially small and gradually increase as you gain experience and confidence. Pay attention to your emotional responses and decision-making patterns.

Step 3: Knowledge Gap Analysis
Identify specific areas where you need additional education or experience. Focus on understanding the instruments you'll use and the market dynamics that will drive opportunities during the intelligence explosion. Don't try to become an expert on everything—develop deep knowledge in your chosen strategies.

Step 4: Emotional Resilience Building Develop specific practices and systems that help you maintain emotional equilibrium during market volatility. This might include meditation, exercise, support groups, or other stress management techniques. The goal is to maintain rational decision-making capacity under pressure.

Step 5: Foundation Stress Testing
Before deploying significant capital, test your foundation with smaller positions during volatile market conditions. Pay attention to how you handle drawdowns, how you make decisions under pressure, and how market movements affect your daily life.

The Foundation Maintenance System
Building your market trading foundation isn't a one-time event—it's an ongoing process that requires regular assessment and adjustment. Market conditions change, your financial situation evolves, and your emotional capacity develops over time.

Monthly Foundation Reviews: Each month, assess your capital allocation, risk tolerance, and emotional state. Are you still comfortable with your position sizes? Have your financial circumstances changed? Are you making rational decisions or letting emotions drive your choices?

Quarterly Stress Tests: Every quarter, examine how you've handled market volatility and whether your foundation remains solid. Look for signs of overextension, emotional decision-making, or deviation from your predetermined strategies.

Annual Foundation Upgrades: Each year, consider whether your foundation can support larger positions or more sophisticated strategies. As your experience and emotional capacity grow, you may be able to handle larger allocations and more complex approaches.

The intelligence explosion represents the wealth-building opportunity of our lifetime, but it demands a foundation strong enough to support the psychological and financial pressures of leveraged market strategies. Those who build solid foundations will capture exponential returns while protecting their downside. Those who skip this crucial step will watch opportunities slip away or, worse, destroy their existing wealth through overextension and emotional decision-making.

Your foundation determines everything that follows. With a solid foundation, you can confidently deploy the FIRE Framework strategies that will build your unbreakable wealth during the intelligence explosion. Without it, you're building on quicksand, and the first major market movement will reveal the weakness in your approach.

Now that you understand your true capacity and have built a solid foundation, you're ready to learn how to recognize and time the market opportunities that will fuel your wealth-building strategy. The next chapter will teach you to read the psychological patterns that drive market cycles and identify the optimal moments to deploy your carefully allocated capital.

Chapter Three

Bubble Psychology and Market Timing

Every fortune is made during chaos, not calm. The AI revolution isn't just changing technology—it's creating one of the largest wealth transfers in human history, and those who understand bubble psychology will capture the lion's share. Most investors watch from the sidelines, paralyzed by fear or blinded by greed, while the few who master market timing during technology explosions secure generational wealth.

Market bubbles aren't random events—they're predictable psychological patterns that repeat with stunning consistency. When you understand how fear and greed drive market cycles, you transform from a reactive investor into a strategic wealth extractor. This chapter will teach you to recognize the distinct phases of AI-driven market bubbles and profit from the emotional decisions of the masses.

The intelligence explosion belongs to those who extract gains to build moats, and mastering bubble psychology is your foundation for doing exactly that.

The Hidden Psychology Behind Bubbles

Financial bubbles follow a predictable emotional cycle that's been documented across centuries of market history. From the Dutch tulip mania to the dot-com boom, the same psychological patterns emerge every time new technology promises to change the world. The AI revolution is no different—it's creating the same emotional responses that drive extraordinary wealth creation and destruction.

The key to profiting from bubbles isn't avoiding them—it's understanding them. Most investors make the fatal mistake of trying to time the peak, but smart money focuses on the corrections. During the dot-com bubble, Amazon stock fell 94% from its peak, yet early investors who bought during the correction became millionaires. The same pattern is playing out with AI-driven companies today.

The Four Phases of Technology Bubbles

Every technology bubble follows the same psychological progression:

1. **Skepticism Phase**: New technology emerges, but most investors dismiss it as hype

2. **Awareness Phase**: Early adopters begin to see potential, prices start rising

3. **Euphoria Phase**: Mainstream media coverage explodes, everyone wants in

4. **Correction Phase**: Reality sets in, weak hands sell, strong companies emerge

Understanding these phases gives you a massive advantage. While others react emotionally to price movements, you'll recognize where you are in the cycle and position yourself accordingly. The AI bubble is currently transitioning from awareness to euphoria—creating the perfect conditions for strategic wealth extraction.

Reading the Emotional Temperature of Markets

Market sentiment is like a thermometer for human psychology. When you learn to read the emotional temperature of AI-driven markets, you'll spot opportunities that others miss. The key is recognizing when sentiment reaches unsustainable extremes in either direction.

Euphoria Indicators to Watch

When markets get too hot, certain warning signs appear:

- **Media Coverage Explosion**: When your barber starts giving stock tips about AI companies
- **Venture Capital Frenzy**: New AI startups raising millions with no revenue
- **Celebrity Endorsements**: Famous people promoting AI investments on social media
- **FOMO-Driven Buying**: People borrowing money to buy AI stocks
- **Valuation Disconnection**: Stock prices completely divorced from fundamentals

These indicators don't mean the bubble is about to burst—they mean it's entering the phase where corrections become more likely. Smart investors use these signals to prepare for the inevitable pullback.

Fear Indicators That Signal Opportunity

When markets get too cold, different signals emerge:
- **Panic Selling**: Massive volume spikes as investors dump positions
- **Negative News Dominance**: Media focusing only on AI failures and risks
- **Insider Buying**: Company executives purchasing their own stock
- **Oversold Technical Conditions**: Price drops that exceed fundamental deterioration
- **Liquidity Crises**: Good companies struggling to raise capital

These fear indicators often create the best buying opportunities. When others are selling in panic, you're positioning for the next wave of growth.

The Three Types of Market Corrections

Not all market corrections are created equal. Understanding the difference between healthy pullbacks, intermediate corrections, and dangerous reversals is crucial for timing your entries and exits effectively.

Healthy Pullbacks (5-10% Decline)

These are the bread and butter of smart market timing. Healthy pullbacks occur when:
- Overall trend remains intact
- Correction lasts 1-4 weeks
- Volume decreases during the decline
- Fundamental factors remain strong
- Technical indicators show oversold conditions

During healthy pullbacks, you want to be buying. These corrections shake out weak hands and create entry opportunities for patient investors. The key is having cash ready and the emotional discipline to act when others are hesitant.

Intermediate Corrections (10-20% Decline)

These corrections require more careful analysis. They occur when:
- Market sentiment shifts from optimism to concern
- Correction lasts 1-3 months
- Some fundamental factors begin to deteriorate

- Technical indicators show mixed signals
- Institutional investors start reducing exposure

Intermediate corrections can be opportunities, but they require more selective buying. Focus on the strongest companies with the best fundamentals and wait for clear signs of stabilization before committing significant capital.

Dangerous Reversals (20%+ Decline)

These are the corrections that destroy wealth if you're not prepared. Warning signs include:

- Fundamental deterioration in the economy or sector
- Credit markets begin to freeze
- Margin calls force widespread selling
- Technical indicators show broad-based weakness
- Insider selling accelerates

During dangerous reversals, preservation of capital becomes the priority. This is when you want to be reducing exposure and waiting for clearer signals before re-entering the market.

Technical Analysis for Bubble Cycles

Technical analysis becomes especially powerful during bubble cycles because it captures the emotional extremes that drive price movements. While fundamental analysis tells you what should happen, technical analysis shows you what is happening in the minds of investors. This analysis can also be applied to different timeframes. For example, your analysis of a monthly chart may lead you to be cautious of a current reversal as you use shorter-term charts to determine when to execute trades.

Key Technical Indicators for Bubble Timing

Moving Averages: The relationship between short-term and long-term moving averages reveals the underlying trend. During healthy markets, prices stay above key moving averages. When prices fall below major moving averages with high volume, it signals a potential correction.

Commodity Channel Index (CCI): This momentum-based oscillator gauges how far a stock's price has moved from its historical average. CCI readings above +100 suggest overbought conditions, while readings below -100 indicate oversold levels. During bubble cycles, CCI can remain elevated or depressed for extended periods, reflecting prolonged investor sentiment extremes.

Relative Strength Index (RSI): This momentum indicator measures whether stocks are overbought or oversold. RSI readings above 70 suggest overbought conditions, while readings below 30 indicate oversold levels. During bubble cycles, RSI can stay at extreme levels longer than normal.

Volume Analysis: Volume patterns reveal the conviction behind price movements. Rising prices on increasing volume suggest strong momentum, while rising prices on decreasing volume indicate weakening support. During corrections, you want to see selling volume decrease as prices stabilize.

Support and Resistance Levels: These psychological price levels act as floors and ceilings for stock prices. During bubble cycles, these levels become especially important as they represent areas where emotional decisions cluster.

The Volume-Price Relationship

Understanding how volume interacts with price movements gives you insight into market psychology. This relationship is especially important during AI-driven market cycles because it reveals the conviction behind price moves.

Accumulation Patterns: When prices rise on increasing volume, it indicates strong buying interest. This pattern suggests institutional investors are building positions, creating a foundation for continued gains. Look for this pattern during market corrections as a sign of emerging strength.

Distribution Patterns: When prices rise on decreasing volume, it suggests selling pressure is increasing. This pattern often precedes corrections as smart money begins to reduce exposure. Recognizing distribution patterns helps you avoid buying at the top of short-term moves.

Climax Patterns: These occur when volume spikes to extreme levels, often coinciding with major price moves. Buying climaxes often mark short-term tops, while selling climaxes frequently signal bottoms. These patterns are especially common during bubble cycles.

Economic Indicators That Confirm Market Timing

Technical analysis becomes more reliable when confirmed by economic indicators. These fundamental measures provide context for market movements and help distinguish between temporary corrections and structural changes.

Leading Economic Indicators

- **Employment Data**: Strong job growth supports consumer spending and market optimism
- **Manufacturing Activity**: Rising production indicates economic expansion
- **Consumer Confidence**: High confidence levels support continued spending
- **Credit Spreads**: Narrow spreads indicate healthy credit markets
- **Yield Curve**: Normal upward slope suggests economic stability

Lagging Economic Indicators

- **Inflation Data**: Rising inflation can pressure stock valuations
- **Corporate Earnings**: Past earnings confirm or contradict market optimism
- **GDP Growth**: Economic growth supports market valuations
- **Unemployment Rate**: Employment trends affect consumer behavior
- **Interest Rates**: Rate changes impact investment attractiveness

The Psychology of Successful Market Timing

Technical analysis and economic indicators are just tools. The real challenge of market timing is psychological. Most investors know what to do—they struggle with when to do it. Success requires developing the emotional discipline to act when conditions are right, even when it feels uncomfortable.

The Paradox of Contrarian Investing

The best buying opportunities feel the worst. When markets are correcting, negative news dominates headlines, and everyone is talking about how bad things are. This is exactly when you want to be buying, but it's also when it feels most dangerous.

Successful market timing requires accepting this paradox. You must be willing to buy when others are selling and sell when others are buying. This goes against every human instinct, which is why so few investors succeed at it.

Developing Emotional Discipline

The key to emotional discipline is preparation. Before market corrections happen, you need to:

1. **Set Clear Criteria**: Define exactly what conditions will trigger your buying decisions

2. **Prepare Your Capital**: Have cash ready to deploy when opportunities arise

3. **Control Position Sizes**: Never risk more than you can afford to lose on any single trade

4. **Plan Your Exits**: Know when you'll take profits and when you'll cut losses

5. **Practice Patience**: Wait for the right opportunities rather than forcing trades

Risk Management During Bubble Cycles

Bubble cycles create extraordinary opportunities, but they also magnify risks. Proper risk management isn't about avoiding risk—it's about taking calculated risks that offer asymmetric returns.

The 2% Rule

Never risk more than 2% of your total capital on any single trade. This rule ensures that even a series of losses won't significantly damage your portfolio. During bubble cycles, when volatility increases, this rule becomes even more important.

Position Sizing Based on Conviction

Not all opportunities are equal. When you have high conviction based on technical and fundamental analysis, you can take larger positions. When uncertainty is high, reduce position sizes accordingly. The key is matching your position size to your confidence level.

Stop-Loss Strategies

Stop-losses protect you from catastrophic losses, but they must be used intelligently. During bubble cycles, normal volatility increases, so stops need to be wider. Consider using percentage-based stops rather than fixed dollar amounts.

Diversification Across Time

Don't put all your capital to work at once. Scale into positions over time, buying more as your thesis is confirmed. This approach reduces the impact of poor timing while allowing you to benefit from market corrections.

Building Your Market Timing System

Successful market timing requires a systematic approach. You can't rely on gut feelings or daily market noise. Instead, you need a repeatable process that removes emotion from your decision-making.

Your Weekly Market Review Process

1. **Analyze Technical Indicators**: Review key charts and momentum indicators

2. **Check Economic Data**: Monitor leading and lagging economic indicators

3. **Assess Market Sentiment**: Evaluate fear and greed levels in the market

4. **Review Your Positions**: Ensure your portfolio aligns with current market conditions

5. **Plan Next Week's Actions**: Identify potential opportunities and risks

Creating Your Watchlist

Maintain a list of high-liquidity investments to monitor and trade. This list should include:

- Broad market index funds
- Sector-specific ETFs
- Leveraged index ETFs
- Individual stocks of AI leaders
- International AI exposure
- Emerging technology themes
- Cryptocurrencies and blockchain investments

Setting Up Alerts

Use technology to monitor your opportunities. Set up alerts for:

- Price levels that would trigger buying interest
- Technical indicator signals
- Economic data releases

- News events that could impact your strategy
- Volume spikes that might signal opportunity

The Intelligence Explosion Advantage

The AI revolution creates unique opportunities for market timing because it's happening faster than previous technology cycles. The acceleration of AI development means bubble cycles are compressed, creating more frequent opportunities for those who understand the patterns.

Why AI Bubbles Are Different

AI bubbles have several unique characteristics:
- **Faster Development Cycles**: AI capabilities improve exponentially, not linearly
- **Broader Economic Impact**: AI affects every industry, not just technology
- **Higher Volatility**: Fear and greed are amplified by AI's transformative potential
- **Global Competition**: Nations and companies compete for AI dominance
- **Regulatory Uncertainty**: Governments struggle to keep up with AI development

These factors create more frequent corrections and more extreme price movements, providing additional opportunities for skilled market timers.

The 10-Year Window

The current AI boom is still in its early stages, but the most explosive growth will likely occur over the next 10 years. This compressed timeline means you need to act quickly to capture the greatest opportunities. The intelligence explosion belongs to those who extract gains to build moats, and this window won't stay open forever.

Preparing for the Next Phase

Market timing during bubble cycles is just the first step in the FIRE Framework. The real wealth is built by taking your market gains and reinvesting them into resilient businesses that can survive and thrive in an AI-dominated economy.

As you develop your market timing skills, remember that the ultimate goal isn't to become a day trader—it's to generate the capital needed to build lasting wealth. Each successful trade should bring you closer to financial independence and the ability to invest in the businesses that will define the next economic era.

The patterns you learn in this chapter will serve you well as we move into the next phase of the FIRE Framework. But first, you need to master the psychological and technical aspects of market timing. The investors who succeed in the intelligence explosion will be those who can remain calm during chaos and act decisively when opportunities arise.

Your journey to unbreakable wealth begins with understanding that markets are driven by human psychology, not just fundamentals. By mastering bubble psychology and market timing, you're positioning yourself to extract maximum value from the AI revolution and build the foundation for lasting financial success.

The next chapter will introduce you to the complete FIRE Framework, showing you how market timing fits into a comprehensive wealth-building system designed specifically for the intelligence explosion. You'll discover how to transform your market timing skills into a systematic approach that compounds your wealth while reducing your risk.

CHAPTER FOUR

MASTERING MARKET CHAOS

OFTEN REGARDED AS "RISK," market volatility becomes your greatest wealth creation tool during the intelligence explosion. While others panic when AI-driven market swings create uncertainty, you'll discover how to systematically convert this chaos into strategic advantage. The FIRE Framework transforms what appears to be random market movements into a predictable wealth extraction system. This chapter reveals why volatility isn't your enemy—it's the key to unlocking exponential returns.

The Intelligence Explosion Creates Unprecedented Opportunity

The current AI revolution represents one of the most significant wealth creation opportunities in human history. Unlike previous technological shifts that unfolded over decades, artificial intelligence is compressing innovation cycles into months and weeks. This acceleration creates massive market dislocations that traditional investment approaches can't capture effectively.

Consider the dot-com boom of the late 1990s. That bubble took nearly five years to fully develop, giving investors multiple entry and exit points. Today's AI explosion is happening at 10x that speed. Companies are gaining billion-dollar valuations in months rather than years. Market capitalizations are swinging by hundreds of billions of dollars in single trading sessions. Indexes are poised are experience exponential gains as productivity skyrockets.

This rapid-fire environment creates two distinct groups of investors. The first group gets overwhelmed by the pace and either sits on the sidelines or makes emotional decisions that destroy wealth. The second group—the one you're joining—uses systematic approaches to profit from the chaos.

The traditional investment playbook breaks down during intelligence explosions. Buy-and-hold strategies become obsolete when entire industries can be disrupted overnight. Diversification provides little protection when AI advancements simultaneously impact every sector. Even professional fund managers struggle because their risk management systems weren't designed for this level of volatility.

The FIRE Framework solves these problems by providing a systematic approach that works specifically during periods of technological disruption. Rather than fighting the volatility, you'll learn to ride it like a professional surfer rides massive waves.

Why Most Investors Fail During Market Explosions

Before we explore the FIRE Framework's advantages, you need to understand why traditional approaches fail during intelligence explosions. This knowledge will help you avoid the common traps that destroy wealth during these periods.

Emotional Decision-Making represents the biggest wealth destroyer during volatile markets. When the S&P 500 drops 5% in a single day due to AI-related fears, most investors panic and sell at the worst possible time. When it rebounds 7% the next day on positive AI news, they miss the recovery entirely.

The human brain isn't wired for the pace of modern markets. We evolved to handle threats that developed over days or weeks, not milliseconds. High-frequency trading algorithms and programmatic investment systems now dominate price discovery, creating market movements that feel random to human observers.

Lack of a Systematic Approach compounds the emotional decision-making problem. Without a clear framework, investors make ad-hoc decisions based on the latest news headline, sudden market movements, or, even worse, emotions. They buy Tesla because of a positive announcement, then sell it the next week when an unrelated headline trashes Elon Musk.

This reactive approach guarantees poor timing. You'll always be one step behind the market rather than positioning ahead of major moves. The FIRE Framework addresses this problem by helping establish clear rules for when to enter and exit positions.

Inadequate Risk Management subtracts more value than poor stock selection, especially during volatile periods. Traditional portfolio theory suggests that diversification reduces risk, but this breaks down when AI developments affect every sector. A 60/40 stock-bond portfolio provides little protection when both stocks and bonds decline together due to technological disruption.

Retail investors often make this worse by using excessive leverage without proper risk controls. They borrow money to amplify returns during good periods, then face margin calls during downturns. The FIRE Framework includes built-in risk management techniques that prevent these catastrophic losses.

The FIRE Framework Advantage Explained

The FIRE Framework provides four distinct advantages that make it uniquely effective during the intelligence explosion. Each component builds upon the previous one to create a wealth multiplication system that thrives on volatility. The foundation lies in extracting gains from public markets during the exponential bubble formations and using the proceeds to establish diversified cash flows resistant to AI upheaval.

Systematic Signal Recognition forms the foundation of the FIRE approach. Rather than relying on gut feelings or news headlines, you'll learn to identify genuine market signals that indicate optimal entry and exit points. This isn't about predicting the future—it's about recognizing patterns that consistently repeat during market cycles.

The Focus component teaches you to identify when broad market indexes are oversold or overbought across various timeframes. These "reversal" moments create opportunities that generate outsized returns when the market returns to trend. You're not trying to pick individual winners—you're capitalizing on systematic overreactions.

Defined-Risk Leverage allows you to amplify returns without risking catastrophic losses. Traditional leverage approaches can wipe out your entire portfolio if markets move against you. The FIRE Framework's Invest component uses financial instruments that provide upside exposure while limiting downside risk to predetermined amounts.

This approach lets you capture exponential gains during market movements while sleeping soundly at night. You'll know exactly how much you can lose on any position before you enter it and many times, never hold a position after hours. This also allows you to size positions appropriately and avoid the emotional decision-making that crushes wealth.

Business Asset Conversion represents the most powerful aspect of the FIRE Framework. While other investors try to time markets indefinitely, you'll learn to convert trading profits into cash-flowing business assets. This creates wealth that compounds independently of financial markets.

The Reinvest component focuses on acquiring businesses that are able to resist as AI dominates the landscape. Rather than betting against AI disruption, you'll own companies that benefit from it or the companies that can't be replaced by it. This strategic shift from market timing to business ownership creates lasting wealth that survives over market cycles.

Diversified Wealth Preservation ensures your gains become permanent rather than temporary. The Endure component teaches you to build multiple income streams that aren't correlated with each other. This creates what Warren Buffett calls "economic moats"—competitive advantages that protect your wealth from future disruption.

Focus: Technical Analysis in Financial Markets

The first component of the FIRE Framework teaches you to identify optimal entry points in trending and volatile markets. This isn't about complicated chart patterns or esoteric indicators—it's about identifying divergences across factors, like price and momentum, and finding fail points.

Reversal Identification requires distinguishing between temporary counter-trend moves and the start of a true directional change. During the intelligence explosion, healthy corrections occur when positive AI developments cause markets to overshoot, then pull back to more reasonable levels. These pullbacks create buying opportunities. The same conditions can also lead to dangerous reversals when markets become overbought and enthusiasm disconnects from reality, triggering a lasting change in trend.

Corrections happen when fundamental problems emerge with AI development or adoption. These might include regulatory crackdowns, technical limitations, or economic disruptions that threaten the AI revolution itself. The Focus component teaches you to distinguish between these scenarios while watching for periods of "irrational exuberance."

Technical indicators help identify these opportunities systematically. The Commodity Channel Index (CCI) and Relative Strength Index (RSI) provide objective measures of when markets become overbought and oversold. When these indicators reach extreme levels, they often signal opportunities for technical investors and traders. However, in the context of the FIRE Framework, indicators help identify divergence and exhaustion.

Economic Confirmation prevents you from catching falling knives during genuine market crashes. Technical analysis alone isn't sufficient—you need economic context to validate your signals. The Focus component teaches you to monitor key economic indicators that affect market mechanics.

Interest rates play a crucial role in company valuations and market movements. When the Federal Reserve raises rates, it increases the cost of capital for companies that rely on heavy investment in research and development. This can trigger market selloffs that create buying opportunities for patient investors.

Employment data provides insight into economic factors outside of company profits. The Focus component teaches you to monitor these trends and adjust your strategy accordingly, avoid trading around announcements altogether, or be poised to act when the market overreacts to breaking news.

Position Sizing Strategy ensures you can withstand market volatility without forced liquidation. Even perfect timing means nothing if you can't hold your positions through temporary adverse movements. The Focus component helps outline specific rules for determining optimal position sizes based on your risk tolerance, market conditions, and confidence levels.

A general rule is never risk more than 2% of your total capital on any single trade. This allows you to be wrong 50 times in a row without wiping out your account. During the intelligence explosion, this conservative approach prevents emotional decision-making that destroys wealth. The Focus component allows you to make adjustments to this general rule as you get comfortable with your strategy and define risk using alternative methods.

Invest: Leveraged Instruments for Maximum Gains

The second component of the FIRE Framework teaches you to deploy leveraged financial instruments that capture broad market gains while limiting downside risk. This approach amplifies returns during AI-driven market surges without exposing you to unlimited losses.

Index Futures Strategy provides the most efficient way to gain leveraged exposure to broad market movements. Rather than trying to pick individual AI winners, you'll profit from the overall economic benefits of artificial intelligence adoption. This diversified approach reduces the risk of betting on specific companies or technologies.

The NASDAQ and S&P 500 futures contracts offer exposure to America's largest companies, most of which benefit from productivity increases. The Nasdaq 100 futures contract offers more concentrated exposure to technology companies that drive innovation. These contracts can be traded for as little as $50 and offer the ability to ratchet up exposure and risk based on your unique tolerance.

Leverage amplifies both gains and losses, so proper risk management is essential. The FIRE Framework uses stop-loss orders in futures trading strategies to limit downside risk to predetermined amounts. This helps to capture exponential gains during favorable market movements while protecting your capital when a trade goes wrong.

Leveraged ETF Implementation provides an alternative to futures trading that's accessible through standard brokerage accounts. These funds use derivatives to amplify market movements, typically providing 2x or 3x the daily return of underlying indices.

The QQQ (Nasdaq 100) has leveraged versions like TQQQ (3x) and QLD (2x) that amplify technology sector gains. The SPY (S&P 500) has leveraged versions like SPXL (3x) and SSO (2x) that amplify broad market gains. These instruments provide leveraged exposure without the complexity of futures trading.

However, leveraged ETFs include built-in decay that makes them unsuitable for long-term holding. The FIRE Framework uses these instruments for short-term tactical positions that capitalize on specific market movements. You'll learn to time entries and exits to maximize gains while minimizing decay effects.

Options Strategies for Defined Risk provide the most sophisticated way to capture leveraged gains with predetermined maximum losses. The FIRE Framework uses specific options strategies that profit from market movements while limiting downside risk to the premium paid.

Call options provide unlimited upside potential with limited downside risk. When you buy a call option on the S&P 500, you profit from market gains above the strike price while limiting losses to the premium paid. This creates asymmetric risk-reward profiles that are ideal for volatile markets.

The key to options success is understanding implied volatility and time decay. The FIRE Framework teaches you to buy options when implied volatility is low and sell them when it's high. This approach captures profits from volatility expansion during market events.

Reinvest: Building Your Business Empire
The third component of the FIRE Framework represents the most powerful wealth creation strategy: converting market profits into cash-flowing business assets. This approach creates wealth that compounds independently of market cycles and provides protection against future economic disruption.

Business Selection Criteria focuses on companies that become more valuable as AI dominates the economy. Rather than fighting technological disruption, you'll own businesses that benefit from it or are immune to it. This strategic approach creates alignment between your investments and the dominant economic trends.

Scalable service businesses represent some of the best opportunities for AI-era investment. These companies can grow revenues without proportional increases in costs, creating expanding profit margins as they scale. Service providers also offer stability during economic transitions. While AI may disrupt many industries, certain services remain necessary regardless of technological changes. Healthcare, legal services, and financial planning represent sectors where human expertise remains valuable even as AI provides supporting tools.

Financial Metrics Analysis ensures you acquire businesses with strong unit economics and growth potential. The FIRE Framework provides specific financial criteria that identify companies positioned for success in the AI-dominated economy.

Revenue growth rates above 20% annually indicate strong market demand and effective business models. Companies growing this rapidly often have products or services that solve important problems for customers. During the AI transition, these businesses often benefit from increased demand for their solutions.

Gross margins above 60% suggest scalable business models that can generate increasing profits as they grow. Software companies often achieve these margins because they can serve additional customers without proportional increases in costs. This scalability becomes more valuable as AI adoption accelerates economic activity.

Customer lifetime value to acquisition cost ratios above 3:1 indicate efficient marketing and strong customer retention. These businesses have proven their ability to profitably acquire customers and generate recurring revenue. This predictability becomes more valuable during volatile economic periods.

Acquisition Strategy focuses on purchasing businesses at reasonable valuations that provide immediate cash flow and long-term growth potential. The FIRE Framework provides specific valuation criteria that ensure you don't overpay for assets, even during competitive markets.

Purchase price multiples between 3-5x annual profits represent fair valuations for small to medium-sized businesses. These multiples provide reasonable returns while allowing for growth upside. During the AI transition, businesses trading at these multiples often provide the best risk-adjusted returns.

Owner financing structures reduce your upfront capital requirements while providing sellers with attractive terms. Many business owners prefer receiving payments over time rather than lump sums, especially if they're concerned about market volatility. This arrangement benefits both parties while conserving your capital for additional opportunities.

Due diligence processes ensure you understand the business's strengths, weaknesses, and growth potential before completing acquisitions. The FIRE Framework provides specific checklists that help you evaluate businesses systematically and avoid costly mistakes.

Endure: Creating Unbreakable Wealth

The fourth component of the FIRE Framework focuses on building diversified wealth that survives economic disruption and generates income for decades. This approach creates true financial independence that doesn't depend on your active involvement or favorable market conditions.

Diversified Income Streams provide stability during economic transitions and protection against industry-specific disruption. The FIRE Framework teaches you to build multiple sources of income that aren't correlated with each other, creating a robust financial foundation.

From existing businesses to new franchise territories and from real estate to other real estate assets, the Endure stage is about finding several avenues of income and efficiently allocating resources to their development.

Legal Structure Optimization protects your assets from potential future risks while minimizing tax obligations. The FIRE Framework provides guidance on establishing proper legal structures that preserve wealth across generations.

Limited liability companies (LLCs) provide asset protection while maintaining operational flexibility. These structures separate your business assets from your personal assets, protecting your wealth from potential lawsuits or business failures. Proper structuring also provides tax advantages that increase your after-tax returns.

Trust structures provide additional asset protection and estate planning benefits. Revocable trusts avoid probate and provide privacy for your estate planning. Irrevocable trusts provide stronger asset protection and can reduce estate taxes for high-net-worth individuals. Tax optimization strategies ensure you keep more of what you earn while remaining compliant with all regulations.

Succession Planning ensures your wealth creation system continues operating effectively even if you're not actively involved. This planning becomes more important as your wealth grows and your business portfolio expands.

Management systems reduce your day-to-day involvement in business operations while maintaining oversight of performance and profitability. Key performance indicators (KPIs) help you monitor business health without micromanaging daily operations. Regular reporting systems keep you informed while allowing managers to operate independently.

Exit strategies provide liquidity options for your business investments when you need capital or want to reduce your involvement. The FIRE Framework teaches you to structure acquisitions with exit strategies in mind, ensuring you can monetize your investments when appropriate.

Estate planning ensures your wealth transfers efficiently to your beneficiaries while minimizing tax obligations. Proper planning protects your family's financial security and preserves the wealth you've created through the FIRE Framework.

The Compound Effect of FIRE Implementation

The true power of the FIRE Framework emerges when all four components work together to create exponential wealth growth. Each component amplifies the others, creating a compound effect that generates wealth far beyond what any single strategy could achieve.

Systematic Wealth Multiplication occurs when your technical analysis skills improve your market timing, your leveraged instruments amplify your gains, your business acquisitions provide steady cash flow, and your diversified holdings protect your wealth. This creates a positive feedback loop that accelerates wealth creation.

The profits from your Focus and Invest strategies provide capital for your Reinvest acquisitions. While the cash flow from your acquired business portfolio is diversified and protected with Endure.

Time Leverage multiplies your wealth creation efforts by building systems that generate returns with or without your direct involvement. This frees your time to focus on the highest-value activities.

As your wealth grows, you can hire professionals to manage various aspects of your portfolio companies. Business brokers can funnel you acquisitions for accountants to analyze, and estate planning attorneys can optimize your legal structures. This professional team amplifies your effectiveness while reducing your workload.

Your Next Steps

You now understand the basics of how the FIRE Framework transforms market volatility into systematic wealth creation during the intelligence explosion. Part II will provide detailed implementation guidance for the FIRE components, teaching you specific skills that will enable you to capitalize on the AI revolution.

Part II: Execute

Rivanna Heights Media

Rivanna Heights Media

Chapter Five

The Psychology of Wealth Extraction

The biggest enemy of wealth creation during the intelligence explosion isn't market volatility or economic uncertainty—it's the human mind. While the FIRE Framework provides the systematic approach to capture AI-driven wealth, your psychological preparation determines whether you'll execute that system effectively or abandon it at the first sign of difficulty. This chapter reveals the mental frameworks that separate successful wealth extractors from those who understand the system but fail to profit from it.

The intelligence explosion creates psychological pressures that didn't exist during previous market cycles. The speed of change, the magnitude of volatility, and the complexity of opportunities create cognitive overload that paralyzes even experienced investors. You'll learn to transform these psychological challenges into competitive advantages through systematic mental preparation.

The Cognitive Warfare of AI Markets

AI-driven markets wage psychological warfare on human participants. High-frequency trading algorithms exploit predictable human emotions, creating market movements designed to trigger fear and greed responses. News cycles compress complex technological developments into simplified narratives that either generate irrational exuberance or apocalyptic fear.

Information Overload represents the first psychological challenge you must overcome. The AI revolution generates exponentially more information than any human can process effectively. Every day brings new breakthrough announcements, regulatory developments, market analyses, and expert predictions. This constant stream creates the illusion that you need to absorb everything to make informed decisions.

The FIRE Framework solves this problem by providing information filters that focus your attention on signals that matter. Instead of trying to process every AI development, you'll learn to identify the specific data points that affect your wealth-building strategy. This selective attention prevents information paralysis while ensuring you don't miss crucial opportunities.

Cognitive Biases become amplified during periods of rapid change. Confirmation bias leads you to seek information that supports your existing beliefs while ignoring contradictory evidence. Recency bias causes you to overweight recent events when making decisions about long-term trends. Loss aversion prevents you from taking calculated risks that could generate exponential returns.

The FIRE Framework includes systematic processes that counteract these biases. You'll use predefined criteria for evaluating opportunities, removing emotional decision-making from your wealth-building process. This systematic approach ensures that profitable opportunities aren't missed due to psychological blind spots.

Decision Fatigue emerges when you're forced to make too many complex decisions in rapid succession. The AI market environment demands constant attention and frequent decision-making, exhausting your mental resources and leading to progressively worse choices throughout the day.

The FIRE Framework minimizes decision fatigue by creating automated systems and clear decision trees. You'll establish rules for when to enter and exit positions, removing the need for constant decision-making. This automation preserves your mental energy for the high-value decisions that truly require your attention.

Building Psychological Resilience for Volatile Markets

Successful wealth extraction during the intelligence explosion requires specific psychological skills that allow you to profit from conditions that destroy less prepared investors. These skills can be developed through systematic practice and mental conditioning.

Emotional Regulation allows you to maintain objective decision-making when markets trigger fear or greed responses. When the NASDAQ drops 10% in a single day due to AI regulation fears, your emotional brain will signal danger and urge you to sell. When it rebounds 15% the next day on positive earnings reports, your emotional brain will signal opportunity and urge you to buy.

Both responses are counterproductive to wealth building. The FIRE Framework teaches you to recognize these emotional triggers and respond with systematic analysis rather than emotional reactions. You'll learn breathing techniques, visualization exercises, and cognitive reframing strategies that maintain psychological equilibrium during market chaos.

Uncertainty Tolerance becomes crucial when operating in rapidly evolving markets where traditional analysis provides limited guidance. The AI revolution creates scenarios that have no historical precedent, making it impossible to predict outcomes with certainty. This uncertainty paralyzes investors who need complete information before making decisions.

The FIRE Framework transforms uncertainty from a liability into an asset. You'll learn to operate effectively with incomplete information, using probability-based thinking rather than certainty-based analysis. This comfort with uncertainty allows you to act decisively when others remain paralyzed by analysis.

Delayed Gratification enables you to execute long-term wealth-building strategies despite short-term market noise. The intelligence explosion creates daily opportunities that appear to offer immediate profits, tempting you to abandon systematic approaches for quick gains.

The FIRE Framework includes specific techniques for maintaining long-term focus despite short-term distractions. You'll learn to visualize long-term outcomes, create milestone rewards, and build accountability systems that keep you focused on systematic wealth building rather than market timing.

The Winner's Mindset: Thinking Like a Wealth Extractor

Successful FIRE Framework implementation requires adopting specific mental models that align your thinking with wealth creation rather than wealth preservation. These mental frameworks separate those who build exponential wealth from those who merely avoid losses.

Abundance Thinking replaces scarcity mindset with the recognition that the intelligence explosion creates unlimited wealth opportunities. Scarcity thinking leads you to hoard cash, avoid calculated risks, and miss opportunities due to fear of loss. Abundance thinking enables you to deploy capital aggressively when opportunities arise.

The FIRE Framework includes exercises that develop abundance thinking through systematic exposure to growth opportunities. You'll learn to calculate expected values, understand risk-reward ratios, and recognize that intelligent risk-taking creates more security than risk avoidance.

Systems Thinking enables you to see connections between different components of your wealth-building strategy. Linear thinking focuses on individual trades or investments, missing the synergies that create exponential wealth. Systems thinking recognizes how Focus improvements enhance Invest returns, how Invest profits fund Reinvest opportunities, and how Reinvest assets support Endure stability.

The FIRE Framework teaches you to optimize your entire wealth-building system rather than individual components. This holistic approach creates compounding effects that generate wealth far beyond the sum of individual strategies.

Contrarian Positioning requires the psychological strength to act when others are paralyzed by fear or intoxicated by greed. The most profitable opportunities during the intelligence explosion occur when markets overreact to news events, creating temporary mispricings that systematic investors can exploit.

The FIRE Framework includes specific techniques for developing contrarian instincts. You'll learn to recognize crowd behavior, identify market overreactions, and position yourself to profit from inevitable corrections. This contrarian approach requires strong psychological conditioning to act against prevailing sentiment.

Developing Your Wealth Extraction Discipline

Discipline separates systematic wealth builders from gamblers who occasionally get lucky. The intelligence explosion creates numerous opportunities for undisciplined speculation that can destroy years of systematic wealth building in days or weeks.

Process Adherence ensures you follow your systematic approach even when emotions suggest deviating from the plan. Markets will create situations where your system signals patience, but breaking news suggests immediate action. Your system will recommend small positions, but apparent opportunities suggest larger bets.

The FIRE Framework includes specific protocols for maintaining process adherence during psychological pressure. You'll create written procedures for common scenarios, establish accountability systems with trusted advisors, and develop self-monitoring techniques that prevent emotional decision-making.

Risk Management Psychology enables you to accept calculated losses as part of systematic wealth building. Many investors understand risk management intellectually but struggle to execute it emotionally. They hold losing positions too long hoping for recoveries, or close profitable positions too early due to fear of giving back gains.

The FIRE Framework teaches you to view individual trades as components of a larger system rather than isolated events. This perspective enables you to accept small losses as the cost of participating in a system that generates larger gains. You'll learn to celebrate good processes rather than individual outcomes.

Continuous Learning Mindset allows you to adapt your approach as markets evolve without abandoning systematic principles. The intelligence explosion creates rapidly changing market conditions that require tactical adjustments to your strategy. However, these adjustments must be systematic rather than emotional.

The FIRE Framework includes structured approaches for evaluating and implementing strategy improvements. You'll learn to distinguish between necessary adaptations and emotional reactions, ensuring your system evolves intelligently rather than randomly.

Performance Psychology: Optimizing Your Execution

Peak performance in wealth extraction requires optimizing your mental and physical state for decision-making. The intelligence explosion creates high-pressure environments where small improvements in execution can generate significant differences in outcomes.

Cognitive Load Management ensures you can process complex information effectively without mental fatigue. The AI market environment demands simultaneous monitoring of technical indicators, economic data, news developments, and portfolio performance. This cognitive load can overwhelm your decision-making capacity if not managed properly.

The FIRE Framework includes specific techniques for optimizing cognitive performance. You'll learn to organize information hierarchically, create decision-making shortcuts, and establish routines that reduce mental strain. These techniques preserve your cognitive resources for high-value decisions.

Attention Control enables you to focus on signals that matter while filtering out distracting noise. The constant stream of market information, news alerts, and social media commentary creates attention fragmentation that reduces decision-making quality.

The FIRE Framework teaches you to create focused work environments, establish information consumption schedules, and develop attention training exercises. This disciplined approach to information consumption improves the quality of your decision-making while reducing stress.

Stress Management maintains optimal performance under pressure. The intelligence explosion creates high-stakes decision-making environments where stress can impair judgment and lead to costly mistakes. Chronic stress also impacts long-term health and decision-making capacity.

The FIRE Framework includes stress management techniques specifically designed for high-pressure investment environments. You'll learn meditation practices, physical exercise routines, and recovery protocols that maintain peak performance during volatile periods.

Building Your Wealth Extraction Support System

No investor succeeds in isolation. The intelligence explosion creates complex challenges that require diverse expertise and perspectives. Building the right support system amplifies your individual capabilities while providing accountability and emotional support.

Professional Advisory Team provides specialized expertise that enhances your decision-making capabilities. This team should include financial advisors familiar with advanced strategies, attorneys experienced in business law, accountants skilled in tax optimization, and insurance professionals who understand asset protection.

The FIRE Framework provides criteria for selecting and managing advisory relationships. You'll learn to evaluate professional competence, establish clear communication protocols, and create accountability systems that ensure you receive value from professional relationships.

Peer Learning Network connects you with other serious wealth builders who can share experiences, provide different perspectives, and offer mutual accountability. This network should include investors with complementary skills, business owners in different industries, and professionals who understand the intelligence explosion.

The FIRE Framework includes strategies for building and maintaining peer networks. You'll learn to identify valuable connections, create mutually beneficial relationships, and establish ongoing communication systems that support long-term wealth building.

Educational Resources ensure you remain current with market developments, technological advances, and wealth-building strategies. The intelligence explosion creates rapidly evolving environments where yesterday's knowledge becomes obsolete quickly.

The FIRE Framework includes systematic approaches for continuous learning. You'll establish information sources, create learning schedules, and develop knowledge management systems that keep you informed without creating information overload.

Your Psychological Preparation Action Plan

Successful FIRE Framework implementation requires systematic psychological preparation that builds the mental skills needed for wealth extraction. This preparation begins before you deploy capital and continues throughout your wealth-building journey.

Phase 1: Foundation Building (Weeks 1-4) focuses on developing basic psychological skills that support systematic wealth building. You'll establish meditation practices, create decision-making protocols, and develop emotional regulation techniques. This foundation enables you to execute your wealth-building strategy without psychological interference.

Phase 2: Skill Development (Weeks 5-12) builds specific psychological skills needed for each FIRE Framework component. You'll develop patience for Focus activities, risk tolerance for Invest strategies, business evaluation skills for Reinvest opportunities, and long-term thinking for Endure planning.

Phase 3: Integration and Optimization (Weeks 13-24) combines psychological skills with systematic wealth-building activities. You'll practice executing your strategy under real market conditions, develop performance feedback systems, and refine your approach based on experience.

Phase 4: Mastery and Scaling (Months 7-24) focuses on optimizing your psychological performance as your wealth-building system scales. You'll develop leadership skills for managing teams, delegation strategies for maintaining oversight, and succession planning for long-term wealth preservation.

The Psychological Edge in AI Markets

The intelligence explosion creates unique psychological challenges that become competitive advantages for properly prepared investors. While others struggle with information overload, decision fatigue, and emotional volatility, you'll use these conditions to extract systematic wealth.

Your psychological preparation transforms market chaos into strategic advantage. When others panic during market downturns, you'll recognize buying opportunities. When others get caught up in speculative bubbles, you'll systematically extract profits. When others abandon their strategies due to short-term setbacks, you'll maintain long-term focus.

The FIRE Framework provides the systematic approach to wealth building, but your psychological preparation determines whether you'll execute that system effectively. This mental conditioning represents the difference between understanding wealth-building principles and actually building wealth.

In the next chapter, we'll explore the specific technical skills needed to implement the Focus component of the FIRE Framework. You'll learn to identify genuine market opportunities with precision, distinguish between temporary corrections and dangerous reversals, and develop the timing skills that turn market volatility into systematic wealth creation.

CHAPTER SIX

FOCUS: TECHNICAL ANALYSIS MASTERY

IN MAY 2010, ONE trader made $1.8 million in eighteen minutes. While algorithms crashed the market faster than any human could react, John Smith (not his real name) watched his technical analysis system flash a simple green 'BUY' signal. Within minutes of the Flash Crash, he was purchasing discounted futures contracts while panic-stricken investors dumped their positions. His success was the result of precise technical analysis that recognized the divergence between price action and momentum indicators. This moment exemplifies how technical analysis mastery can turn market chaos into wealth-building opportunities.

Now, imagine that same opportunity multiplied by the scale of the intelligence explosion. The Flash Crash was a single day of extreme volatility. The expanding market transformation we're experiencing will create similar opportunities weekly, sometimes daily, for those who understand how to read the signals. This chapter will equip you with the technical analysis skills that separate the prepared from the panicked, the profitable from the broke.

Technical analysis during the intelligence explosion is about more than making money—it's about positioning yourself to capture the most significant wealth-building opportunities in human history.

Why Technical Analysis Works in Volatile Markets

Many investors dismiss technical analysis as 'fortune telling with charts.' This misconception costs them millions. The truth is that technical analysis works because it measures what markets actually do, not what they should theoretically do. In expanding markets, this becomes even more powerful because AI systems create recognizable patterns as they process information and execute trades.

When you understand how to read these patterns, you're essentially reading the 'footprints' of algorithmic trading systems. These systems don't trade randomly—they follow programmed logic that creates predictable patterns in price, volume, and momentum. These patterns become your roadmap to profit.

Here's what makes technical analysis so effective during bubbles like the intelligence explosion:

Market Efficiency is a Myth: Traditional finance teaches that markets are efficient, meaning all information is instantly priced in. But markets during times of rapid technological advancement create temporary inefficiencies as traders process new information at different speeds. Technical analysis helps you identify these inefficiencies before they close.

Pattern Recognition Scales: Across timeframes, asset classes, and market structures, recurring dynamics emerge with consistent form and function. The same recurring dynamics—fear, greed, accumulation, distribution—manifest whether you're looking at minutes or months. In speculative phases like bubbles, the patterns may amplify in speed and magnitude, but the principles remain unchanged.

Volume Tells the Story: In bubble-formation markets, volume patterns become incredibly revealing. When AI systems start accumulating or distributing positions, they create volume signatures that technical analysis can detect days or weeks before the price movement becomes obvious.

The Three Pillars of Technical Analysis

To understand the technical analysis used in this framework, you must understand three fundamental concepts: divergence analysis, pattern recognition, and economic confirmation. These three pillars work together to create a comprehensive system for timing market entries with precision.

Think of these three pillars as the foundation of a skyscraper. Without a solid foundation, the tallest building will eventually collapse. Similarly, without mastering these three elements, your market timing will be based on guesswork rather than systematic analysis.

Divergence Analysis: The Hidden Signals

Divergence analysis is the most powerful tool in your technical analysis toolkit. It reveals when the market is about to change direction before the price movement becomes obvious. Most importantly, it works consistently in expanding markets because it measures the underlying strength or weakness of price movements.

Understanding Divergence Patterns

Divergence occurs when price moves in one direction while a momentum indicator moves in the opposite direction. This signals that the current price trend is losing strength and may soon reverse. This technique becomes incredibly powerful during expansions because markets often "overshoot," and create these divergence patterns before major directional changes.

There are two types of divergence patterns you need to master.

Bullish Divergence: This occurs when price makes a lower low while a momentum indicator make a higher low. This pattern suggests that selling pressure is weakening and a price reversal to the upside is likely. In the example below, you can see that the price decline is trending opposite the Commodity Channel Index (CCI).

Bearish Divergence: This occurs when price makes a higher high while a momentum indicator makes a lower high. This pattern suggests that buying pressure is weakening and a price reversal to the downside is likely. In the chart below, you can see the price continues to trend higher while the CCI fails to make new highs.

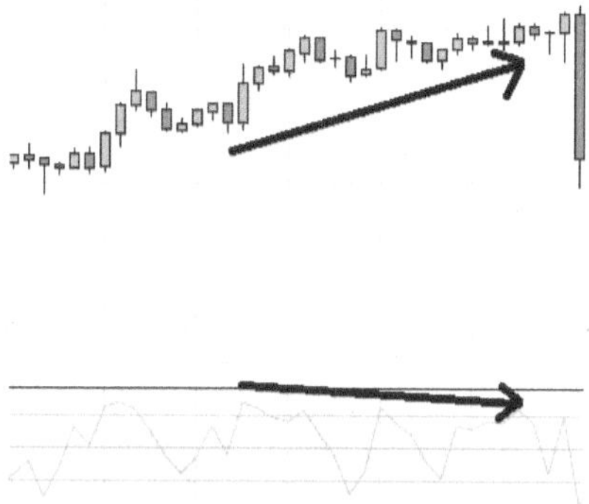

The CCI (Commodity Channel Index) Advantage

The CCI is particularly effective in expanding markets because it measures how far price has deviated from its average. Markets often overreact and create deviations that revert to the mean, making CCI an excellent tool for identifying these opportunities.

Here's how traders typically use CCI:

1. Look for Extreme Readings: CCI readings above +100 or below -100 indicate potential reversal zones. In expanding markets, these extremes often mark the points where algorithmic buying or selling is exhausted.

2. Confirm with Price Action: When CCI reaches extreme readings, look for price to create a corresponding high or low. If price continues in the same direction while CCI moves in the opposite direction, you've identified a divergence.

3. Time Your Entry: The best entry points come when CCI begins to move back toward zero from extreme readings while price starts to follow. This is typically the moment when the divergence starts to resolve with price movement. Another way to time your entry is to watch for failed attempts in the price trend.

The RSI (Relative Strength Index) Precision

RSI is another powerful indicator for divergence analysis because it measures the speed and magnitude of price changes. In expanding markets, RSI becomes particularly useful because it can detect when algorithmic trading is creating unsustainable price moves.

Here's how traders typically use RSI:

1. Focus on the 30-70 Range: While traditional RSI analysis uses 30 and 70 as oversold and overbought levels, in expanding markets, the most reliable divergences occur when RSI moves from these levels back toward 50.

2. Multiple Timeframe Analysis: Check RSI divergences on multiple timeframes. A divergence that appears on both 1-hour and 4-hour charts is more reliable than one that appears on only one timeframe.

3. Volume Confirmation: Strong divergences are often accompanied by changes in volume. When RSI shows a divergence and volume confirms the pattern, your probability of success increases significantly.

Using these two indicators in tandem helps minimize the number of potential trades. They also act to confirm each other. Furthermore, identifying trends in the indicators (as opposed to relying on the extremes typically used by traders) is more effective in identifying price reversals. For example, if the price continues to make new highs, but both CCI and RSI are not, price is likely running out of momentum.

Pattern Recognition: The Market's Language

Chart patterns are the market's way of communicating its intentions. In rapidly expanding markets, these patterns become even more reliable because high-frequency trading creates repeatable formations as information is processed and trades are executed at alarming speed. Learning to read these patterns is like learning to speak the market's native language.

High-Probability Reversal Patterns

Some chart patterns are more reliable than others, especially in expanding markets. Here are the patterns that consistently produce profitable opportunities:

Double Bottoms and Tops: These patterns occur when price tests a support or resistance level twice and fails to break through. In expanding markets, these often represent points where algorithmic support or resistance is strongest. The key is to identify when the pattern is complete and enter before the breakout occurs.

Head and Shoulders: This pattern represents a change in trend direction and is particularly reliable in expanding markets. The pattern consists of three peaks (or troughs for inverse head and shoulders), with the middle peak being the highest (or lowest for inverse).

When this pattern completes, it often signals the beginning of a significant move in the opposite direction.

Ascending and Descending Triangles: These patterns show consolidation before a breakout. In expanding markets, these triangles often form as algorithms accumulate or distribute positions. The key is to identify the pattern early and position yourself for the breakout.

These are important patterns to know, understand, and recognize. You may trade on them or you may use them to understand other traders' mentality. However, analyzing past charts to identify less mainstream charts will be key to your success in momentum trading. The key is to find something that occurs frequently and is not a well-known pattern. This will allow you to exploit the pattern potentially into perpetuity. The chart pattern used to confirm this framework (shown below) is based on one extreme candle, followed, not directly but within two cycles, by two more extreme candles (e.g., a lower candle than the adjacent, followed relatively quickly by two lower candles). This pattern, paired with supporting momentum divergence, can lead to a high success rate.

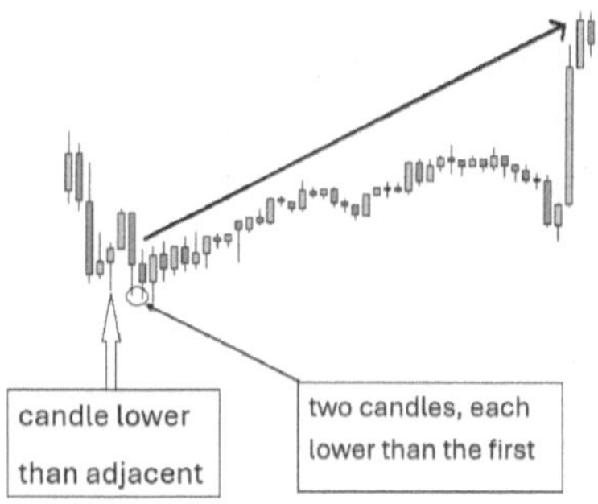

Support and Resistance Mastery

Support and resistance levels are price levels where buying or selling pressure is concentrated. In expanding markets, these levels become incredibly important because they often represent points where traditional trading systems are programmed to act.

Here's how to identify and use support and resistance effectively:

Previous Highs and Lows: These are the most obvious support and resistance levels. In expanding markets, these levels often hold because many algorithms are programmed to respect these historical levels.

Moving Averages: The 50-day and 200-day moving averages often act as dynamic support and resistance. In expanding markets, these are particularly important because many algorithms use moving averages as reference points.

Psychological Levels: Round numbers like 100, 1000, or 10,000 often act as support and resistance. This is because many algorithms are programmed to recognize these levels, and human traders also tend to place orders near these levels.

Volume Analysis: The Truth Behind Price

Volume is the fuel that drives price movements. In expanding markets, volume patterns become incredibly revealing because they show when algorithmic systems are actively buying or selling. Learning to read volume patterns is essential for confirming your technical analysis signals.

Here are the key volume patterns to watch:

Volume Spikes: Sudden increases in volume often precede significant price moves. In expanding markets, these spikes often indicate that algorithmic systems are reacting to new information or reaching programmed trigger points.

Volume Climax: This occurs when volume reaches extremely high levels and then drops dramatically. This often marks the end of a price move and the beginning of a reversal. In expanding markets, volume climax often indicates that algorithmic buying or selling is exhausted.

Volume Divergence: When price makes a new high or low but volume doesn't confirm the move, it suggests that the price move is weak and could potentially reverse. This is particularly reliable in expanding markets because it indicates that algorithmic support for the move is lacking.

Economic Confirmation: The Reality Check

While technical analysis provides the timing, economic indicators provide the context. In expanding markets, economic confirmation becomes even more important because it helps you distinguish between temporary algorithmic noise and genuine market movements driven by fundamental changes.

Key Economic Indicators for AI-Era Trading

Different economic indicators become important during the intelligence explosion. Here are the most crucial ones to monitor:

AI Adoption Metrics: Track metrics like AI patent applications, AI startup funding, and AI job postings. These indicators provide insight into the real pace of AI adoption and help you understand whether expanding market movements are based on genuine progress or speculation.

Technology Sector Performance: Monitor the performance of technology ETFs like XLK or QQQ. These indexes often lead broader market movements during technology-driven expansions like the intelligence explosion.

Interest Rate Environment: Growth companies are particularly sensitive to interest rate changes. Monitor Federal Reserve communications and interest rate futures to understand the monetary policy environment.

Global Economic Stability: Expanding markets can be particularly volatile during periods of global economic uncertainty. Monitor indicators like the VIX (volatility index) and global economic growth rates to understand the broader context.

Integration Strategy: Combining Technical and Economic Analysis

The most powerful approach combines technical analysis with economic confirmation. Here's how to create an integrated analysis system:

1. Start with Economic Context: Before analyzing any chart, understand the broader economic environment. This helps you understand whether technical patterns are likely to be supported by fundamental factors.

2. Use Technical Analysis for Timing: Once you understand the economic context, use technical analysis to time your entries and exits. This combination gives you both the 'why' and the 'when' of market movements. It is also helpful to analyze several time periods. Starting from longer periods (monthly or weekly) identify the trend, and then move into shorter periods (hour, 15-minute, 5-minute) to confirm your entry.

3. Confirm with Multiple Indicators: Never rely on a single indicator. Use multiple technical indicators and confirm them with economic data to increase your probability of success.

4. Monitor AI-Specific Metrics: Pay special attention to AI-specific economic indicators like patent filings, research funding, and regulatory developments. These can provide early warning of changes that will affect expanding markets. There are several AI newsletters available to help stay informed about market developments.

Creating Your Technical Analysis System

To implement these concepts effectively, you need a systematic approach. Here's how to create a comprehensive technical analysis system for the intelligence explosion:

Daily Analysis Routine

Successful technical analysis requires consistent daily review. Here's a proven routine:

Morning Review (15 minutes):

- Check overnight developments in market news
- Review major economic indicators scheduled for release
- Analyze overnight price action in financial markets
- Identify key support and resistance levels for the day
- Set alerts for key index levels

Market Hours Monitoring (ongoing):

- Watch for divergence patterns as they develop
- Monitor volume patterns for confirmation
- Track economic releases and their immediate market impact
- Look for chart pattern breakouts or breakdowns

Evening Analysis (30 minutes):

- Review the day's price action for pattern development
- Update your charts with new support and resistance levels
- Plan potential setups for the next day
- Review your trading decisions and learn from any mistakes

Setting Up Your Charts

Your chart setup is crucial for effective technical analysis. Here's how to configure your charts for maximum effectiveness:

Timeframe Selection: Use multiple timeframes to get a complete picture. For swing trading during the intelligence explosion, focus on:

- Daily and weekly charts for overall trend direction
- 2-hour charts for confirming price trends

- 30-minute charts (or less) for precise entry points
- A trend will generally be more reliable the longer the time period

Indicator Configuration: Use a combination of trend-following and momentum indicators:
- RSI, CCI, and MACD (or choose others)
- Volume for support
- Money Flow Indicator or other for support
- Analyze different time settings to find repeatable patterns

Common Mistakes to Avoid

Even experienced traders make mistakes with technical analysis. Here are the most common errors to avoid:

Over-Analysis: Don't try to use every indicator available. Focus on a few reliable indicators and master them thoroughly.

Ignoring Volume: Price movements without volume confirmation are often false signals. Always confirm your technical analysis with volume patterns.

Forcing Trades: Not every chart pattern is worth trading. Wait for high-probability setups with clear risk/reward ratios. Make rules and stick to them. Nothing will destroy your bankroll quicker than lack of discipline.

Ignoring Market Context: Technical analysis works best when combined with an understanding of broader market conditions and economic factors.

The Path Forward

Technical analysis mastery is a journey, not a destination. As markets continue to evolve, your analytical skills must evolve as well. The key is to maintain a disciplined approach while remaining flexible enough to adapt to new market conditions.

Remember that technical analysis is the foundation of the Focus step in the FIRE Framework. Without the ability to identify optimal entry points, the other steps become much less effective. Master these skills, and you'll be positioned to capture the maximum profit from the intelligence explosion's market opportunities.

By implementing the divergence analysis, pattern recognition, and economic confirmation techniques outlined in this chapter, you'll have the tools necessary to time market entries with precision. This skill will serve as your competitive advantage as the intelligence explosion creates unprecedented opportunities for wealth creation.

Chapter Seven

Invest: Leveraged Market Instruments

Most market participants don't understand that investors make only one choice when making an investment: How much leverage to use. You are either out or in, and the level of the investment can be ratcheted up based on the opportunity. The intelligence explosion is creating a rare market environment where leveraged instruments become essential tools for wealth multiplication. While traditional investors limit themselves to standard equity exposure, this chapter explores financial instruments that amplify your gains while limiting risk. The "Invest" phase of the FIRE Framework becomes your systematic approach to extracting maximum wealth from the AI-driven market expansion while protecting your capital through intelligent risk management.

Understanding Leveraged Instruments

Traditional investment wisdom preaches patience, diversification, and long-term holding strategies. These approaches work during stable market conditions but fail spectacularly during revolutionary technological shifts. The intelligence explosion creates unprecedented market dynamics that require entirely different tools and strategies.

Leveraged instruments amplify your market exposure, allowing you to capture larger gains from smaller price movements. When markets expand upward by 15%, a 2x leveraged ETF delivers 30% returns on the same capital. When you time these moves correctly using the technical analysis skills from Chapter 6, you multiply your wealth-building velocity during the most profitable market conditions in history.

The key distinction separates intelligent leverage from reckless speculation. Intelligent leverage uses mathematical position sizing, defined risk parameters, and systematic entry/exit strategies. Reckless speculation ignores risk management, uses emotional decision-making, and lacks systematic frameworks for wealth preservation. This difference becomes the foundation upon which all your leveraged investment decisions must rest.

Deploying Index Futures and Leveraged ETFs

The first component of your leveraged investment strategy focuses on capturing broad market movements during AI-driven growth phases. Index futures and leveraged ETFs provide the most efficient vehicles for this exposure without requiring individual stock selection or sector-specific expertise. These instruments become your primary weapons for extracting wealth from market-wide artificial intelligence adoption.

Index futures contracts represent agreements to buy or sell market indexes at predetermined prices on future dates. During the intelligence explosion, certain indexes become more responsive to AI-driven expansion than others. Your selection criteria doesn't focus on AI sensitivity, but on choosing indexes with high liquidity. Liquidity requirements demand selecting only futures contracts with daily trading volumes exceeding 10,000 contracts to ensure efficient entry and exit execution. Furthermore, liquidity also ensures optimal charting patterns are available and reliable. Margin efficiency should also be considered, with a focus on contracts requiring margin deposits that fit your criteria while maintaining exposure to your target market segments.

Your maximum risk per futures contract should never exceed 2% of your total trading capital. This 2% represents the actual dollar amount you could lose if stopped out, not the margin requirement or notional contract value. With $50,000 in trading capital, your maximum risk per futures contract becomes $1,000. The number of contracts you can trade depends on your stop-loss distance from entry - if your stop-loss would create a $500 loss per contract, you could trade two contracts while staying within your 2% risk limit.

Leveraged ETFs provide an alternative to futures contracts with different risk and reward characteristics. These instruments use financial derivatives to amplify index movements by predetermined multiples, whether 2x, 3x, or inverse positions. QQQ leveraged products capture technology sector growth during AI expansion, while UPRO provides broad market exposure with maximum leverage. TQQQ and SQQQ offer the highest leverage at 3x with acceptable liquidity, and SPXL provides a balanced approach to leveraged broad market exposure. It is important to understand wash sale rules when using ETFs in your trading strategy. A **wash sale** occurs when you sell a security at a loss and then buy the same or a substantially identical security within 30 days before or after the sale.

Position sizing for leveraged ETFs requires different risk management approaches than futures contracts. For 2x leveraged ETFs, maintain a maximum of 15% of portfolio per position, while 3x leveraged ETFs should never exceed 10% of portfolio per position. Inverse leveraged ETFs serve as a way to gain short exposure to a security without executing an actual short sale, which typically requires substantially more margin, and they should have the same position sizing limits as leveraged long ETFs.

Directional Options Strategies

Options strategies provide the most sophisticated approach to capturing market moves while establishing predetermined risk parameters. These instruments allow you to profit from correctly identified directional market movements while limiting potential losses to known amounts upfront. This creates an ideal vehicle for intelligent speculation by allowing a "set it and forget it" approach. Once you've identified the direction and structured your position, the trade practically manages itself within defined profit and loss boundaries.

Technical analysis provides the foundation for identifying market reversals and directional moves, but capturing maximum profit from these insights requires sophisticated position structuring. Directional options strategies allow you to amplify returns substantially beyond the underlying market movement while establishing predetermined risk limits. When your technical analysis correctly identifies a reversal, these strategies can multiply your gains far beyond what direct investment in the underlying asset would provide.

Options Fundamentals

An option is a contract that gives you the right, but not the obligation, to buy or sell a stock at a specific price within a certain timeframe. This simple concept creates powerful leverage opportunities when combined with technical analysis insights.

Call options give you the right to buy a stock at a predetermined price (the strike price) before expiration. If you believe technical analysis indicates a stock will rise from $50 to $60, you can purchase a call option with a $52 strike price for perhaps $2. If the stock reaches $60, your option becomes worth $8 (the difference between the stock price and strike price), generating a 300% return while the stock only moved 20%.

Put options work in reverse, giving you the right to sell a stock at the strike price. When technical analysis signals a downward move, put options amplify your profit potential. If that same $50 stock declines to $40, a put option with a $48 strike purchased for $2 becomes worth $8, again creating substantial leverage from the directional move.

The beauty of options lies in defined risk—your maximum loss equals the premium you pay upfront. Unlike short selling or futures contracts, you cannot lose more than your initial investment, making position sizing straightforward and risk management precise without the need for stop-loss orders.

Understanding Basic Options Mechanics

Two fundamental concepts drive the profitability of options: delta and theta. Delta measures how much an option's price changes relative to the underlying asset's movement—a delta of 0.50 means the option gains $0.50 for every $1 move in the stock. Theta represents time decay, showing how much value the option loses each day as expiration approaches. Successful directional trading maximizes delta exposure while managing theta decay through proper timing and strategy selection.

Additional options metrics, known as the Greeks, exist and merit study for deeper understanding, but given the short-term nature of directional trading, delta and theta remain paramount. Volatility also significantly contributes to option pricing—decreasing volatility drives option prices down, regardless of underlying price movement. While the FIRE framework focuses on directional moves rather than volatility prediction, understanding this dynamic creates additional profit opportunities. Volatility typically increases as prices decline, making downside directional plays particularly attractive when technical analysis indicates bearish reversals.

Long Call Strategies for Bullish Reversals

When technical analysis indicates a bullish reversal, long call strategies provide the most direct way to amplify upward moves. This approach offers unlimited upside potential with risk limited to the premium paid. The strategy works best when you expect significant movement within a specific timeframe, making it ideal for breakout patterns, oversold bounce setups, or momentum reversals.

Execution requires selecting strike prices at-the-money or slightly out-of-the-money for maximum leverage, choosing expiration dates with 45-90 days to allow sufficient time for the move to develop, and timing entry to coincide with technical breakout signals or reversal confirmations. Consider a scenario where technical analysis identifies a bullish reversal in a $50 stock. Purchasing call options with a $52.50 strike for $2.00 creates a position where a move to $60 generates a 275% return on the options versus 20% on the stock.

Long Put Strategies for Bearish Reversals

Bearish technical signals call for long put strategies that profit from declining markets. This approach provides substantial leverage on downward moves while limiting risk to the premium paid. The strategy excels during breakdown patterns, overbought corrections, or trend reversal signals where significant downside movement is anticipated.

Implementation focuses on selecting puts at-the-money or slightly out-of-the-money to maximize sensitivity to price declines, timing purchases to align with technical breakdown confirmations, and managing positions to capture the majority of expected moves before time decay accelerates. A practical example involves identifying a bearish reversal in a $100 stock through technical analysis. Purchasing put options with a $95 strike for $3.00 creates substantial profit potential if the stock declines to $85, generating over 200% returns on the options position.

Call Spread Strategies for Controlled Bullish Exposure

Bull call spreads provide directional exposure with reduced cost and defined risk parameters. This strategy involves buying lower strike calls while selling higher strike calls, creating a position that profits from upward movement while capping both maximum gain and loss. The approach works exceptionally well when technical analysis suggests moderate bullish moves rather than explosive breakouts.

Bull spread construction requires buying call options at or near the current stock price, selling call options at target price levels indicated by technical analysis, and selecting expiration dates that provide adequate time for the anticipated move. The net cost represents maximum loss, while maximum profit equals the difference between strikes minus the net premium paid. This structure allows for higher probability trades with favorable risk-reward ratios when technical signals suggest measured upward moves.

Put Spread Strategies for Controlled Bearish Exposure

Bear put spreads offer directional downside exposure with defined risk and reduced capital requirements. This strategy combines buying higher strike puts with selling lower strike puts, creating positions that profit from declining markets while maintaining controlled risk profiles. The approach aligns well with technical patterns suggesting measured declines rather than dramatic crashes.

Construction involves buying put options above the current market price, selling put options at technical support levels or downside targets, and managing the spread to maximize profit as the underlying moves toward the target zone. The net premium paid represents maximum risk, while maximum profit occurs when the stock trades below the lower strike at expiration.

Calculating Position Sizing

The simplest approach to position sizing remains never risking more than you are willing to lose on a single trade. This allows you to remain comfortable with the position regardless of outcome, preventing the emotional decision-making that destroys leveraged trading accounts during volatile periods.

For more sophisticated risk management, the optimal position size follows the Kelly Criterion framework with practical modifications for volatile markets: maintain maximum position size of 5% of total capital per trade, aggregate leverage limit of 25% of portfolio in leveraged instruments, and correlation adjustments by reducing position sizes for correlated trades. This mathematical approach provides objective guidelines when emotions run high.

Every leveraged position requires predetermined profit targets and stop-loss levels before execution. The minimum acceptable risk-reward ratio should align with your historical trading statistics. For example, a strategy with 60% success rate might employ a 1:2 risk-reward ratio, risking one point to gain two points. Lower success rates require wider profit targets (1:3 or 1:4 ratios) to maintain long-term profitability, while higher success rates allow for tighter ratios but should never go below 1:1.

Advanced Techniques for Maximum Profit

Beyond basic instrument deployment, advanced techniques maximize your profit potential during intelligence explosion phases while maintaining strict risk controls. Market volatility increases during technological transitions, creating opportunities to profit from price swings rather than directional movements. Volatility harvesting captures these swings systematically by identifying high volatility periods using VIX readings above 25 as entry signals, deploying straddle strategies that buy both calls and puts on market indices, profiting from large moves regardless of market direction, and managing time decay by closing positions before significant deterioration.

Pairs trading involves simultaneous long and short positions in correlated assets. During AI-driven market phases, certain sector relationships become predictable and profitable. Effective pairs for AI markets include long technology versus short utilities to capture AI adoption versus traditional sectors, long large cap versus short small cap to benefit from flight to quality during uncertainty, and long growth versus short value to profit from growth premium during innovation cycles.

Dynamic hedging adjusts position sizes and hedging ratios based on market conditions and volatility levels. This approach maximizes returns during favorable conditions while increasing protection during adverse periods. During low volatility periods when VIX remains below 20, reduce hedging to 10-15% of portfolio. Medium volatility periods with VIX between 20-30 require increasing hedging to 25-35% of portfolio. High volatility periods with VIX above 30 demand maximum hedging at 40-50% of portfolio.

Essential Risk Management Protocols

Leveraged instruments amplify both gains and losses, making risk management protocols essential for long-term success. These systems protect your capital during adverse market conditions while allowing maximum profit extraction during favorable periods. Leveraged positions sometimes require predetermined exit points to prevent catastrophic losses, with stop-loss levels based on technical analysis rather than arbitrary percentages.

For futures contracts, check key support and resistance levels and place stops 2-3% from these levels if they are closer than your calculated risk-reward ratio stops. Leveraged ETFs require wider 8-12% stops due to their higher underlying volatility and daily rebalancing effects. Options strategies generally don't require traditional stops since risk is limited to the premium paid, but profit-taking stops can be set at 50% of the premium collected or paid to lock in gains. These mathematical parameters remove emotion from exit decisions and preserve capital for future opportunities.

Leveraged positions also require active monitoring due to their amplified price movements. Establish systematic review processes to ensure positions remain aligned with your strategy through daily monitoring protocols:
- Review overnight news affecting your positions
- Check technical indicators for trend changes
- Monitor volatility levels and adjust hedging accordingly
- Assess correlation changes between positions
- Verify margin requirements remain adequate

Market conditions can change rapidly during technological transitions, making emergency exit procedures essential for quick position liquidation when necessary. Exit trigger events include technical breakdown (when price breaks from major support or resistance levels), fundamental changes from major policy announcements, margin calls when available capital drops below safety thresholds, and correlation breakdown when position relationships change unexpectedly.

Preparing for Wealth Multiplication

The profits generated from your leveraged investment strategies provide the capital for the next phase of the FIRE Framework. As you master these instruments and generate consistent returns, you'll accumulate the resources necessary to transition from market participant to business owner. Your leveraged investment success creates a foundation for permanent wealth through business acquisition and ownership. These skills remain valuable throughout your wealth-building journey as they apply to many aspects of business ownership and management.

The systematic approach to risk management, position sizing, and profit extraction that you develop in this phase directly translates to evaluating business opportunities and managing entrepreneurial ventures. Mathematical precision, emotional control, and systematic decision-making—the disciplines required to execute leveraged strategies successfully—become essential for the business selection and acquisition processes that follow. Your ability to calculate risk-reward ratios, manage multiple positions simultaneously, and maintain strict exit disciplines prepares you for the complexities of business ownership that represent the ultimate wealth-building vehicle during the intelligence explosion.

Chapter Eight

Reinvest: Scalable Business Selection

The most successful investors don't just ride market waves—they build their own. In the midst of the intelligence explosion, while others chase the next shiny AI stock, you'll be constructing something far more valuable: a portfolio of businesses that don't just survive disruption but thrive in the face of it. This isn't about speculating on the latest trend; it's about identifying the fundamental characteristics that make businesses unstoppable in an AI-dominated world. The difference between temporary gains and lasting wealth lies in your ability to recognize and capitalize on these patterns.

The Scalability Advantage

Here's what most investors miss: true wealth isn't built by finding undervalued assets—it's created by identifying businesses that can grow exponentially without proportional increases in costs. Traditional businesses hit natural limits. You need more staff to serve more customers. You need bigger facilities to produce more products. You need more managers to oversee more operations. But scalable businesses break these constraints in ways that create exponential value.

Consider how a regional plumbing franchise can transform from a single-truck operation to a multi-market enterprise. The initial investment covers trucks, tools, and trained technicians for one service area. But the business model allows expansion into adjacent territories using the same systems, training protocols, and brand recognition. Each new market requires minimal additional infrastructure while leveraging existing operational knowledge. The cost to serve the tenth market is substantially lower than the first, while revenue compounds across all territories.

This scalability pattern applies across service-based businesses where established systems, training programs, and brand recognition can be replicated in new markets without rebuilding the entire operational foundation.

The businesses that will dominate the next decade share three core characteristics:

1. **Systematic Operations**: They have documented processes and training systems that can be replicated across locations and market
2. **Network Effects**: Each new location or customer makes the overall business more valuable through shared resources, referrals, and operational efficiencies
3. **Defensible Positioning**: They operate in industries where human judgment, local relationships, or regulatory requirements create natural barriers to disruption

When evaluating potential acquisitions, prioritize businesses in sectors that remain fundamentally human-centric. Healthcare services that require personal care, professional services built on trust and expertise, education focused on mentorship and guidance, and local businesses with strong community ties represent some of the most defensible scalable opportunities. These industries benefit from technological enhancement while maintaining their essential human elements.

Financial Metrics That Reveal Scalable Potential

Most investors look at revenue growth and call it a day. But scalable businesses reveal themselves through specific financial signatures that traditional analysis often misses. You need to become fluent in these metrics because they're the early warning system for sustainable growth potential.

Customer acquisition cost (CAC) vs. lifetime value (LTV) forms the foundation of scalable business analysis. The nuanced approach involves examining businesses where this ratio improves over time, not just seeking a healthy static ratio. The most valuable scalable businesses simultaneously reduce their acquisition costs through referrals and reputation while increasing customer lifetime value through repeat business and expanded services.

Gross margin expansion reveals critical scalability patterns. Traditional businesses often experience margin compression as they scale due to increased complexity and competition. Scalable service businesses demonstrate the opposite trend—margins expand with growth because fixed costs like training systems, operational procedures, and brand development distribute across more locations while variable costs per job remain relatively stable.

Operating leverage provides the clearest indicator of scale potential. Calculate the percentage increase in operating income for each percentage increase in revenue. Scalable service businesses typically show operating leverage ratios above 1.3, meaning every dollar of additional revenue generates more than $1.30 in additional operating income once systems are established.

Location productivity metrics measure how efficiently each location or service area converts operational capacity into revenue. Scalable businesses show consistent performance across locations, indicating that their systems and training translate effectively to new markets. Look for businesses where newer locations achieve productivity levels similar to established ones within 12-18 months.

Cash flow predictability indicates how reliably a business can forecast its financial performance, which is essential for scalable businesses that need to make large capital commitments for expansion. Predictable cash flows allow management to confidently invest in new locations, knowing they can accurately project returns and funding requirements. Businesses with erratic, unpredictable cash flows struggle to scale effectively because they cannot reliably plan major growth initiatives.

Identifying Resilient Business Models

As artificial intelligence reshapes entire industries, certain business models will prove more resilient than others. The goal is identifying businesses that operate in sectors where human interaction, physical presence, or specialized expertise remains essential, making them difficult to automate or disrupt.

Physical service requirements create natural barriers to automation. Businesses requiring on-site diagnosis, manual repairs, or hands-on problem-solving maintain competitive advantages. Plumbing, electrical work, HVAC services, and home maintenance involve complex physical environments where human adaptability and real-time decision-making remain superior to automated solutions. When evaluating these opportunities, examine businesses that combine technical expertise with unpredictable problem-solving scenarios.

Personal care and human connection represent sectors where emotional intelligence and interpersonal skills drive value creation. Healthcare services involving patient care, senior assistance, childcare, and personal grooming rely on human judgment, empathy, and adaptability. These businesses can integrate technology for scheduling and operations while preserving their fundamentally human service delivery model.

Regulatory and compliance-heavy operations face slower technological adoption due to safety requirements, licensing restrictions, and liability concerns. Professional services requiring certified expertise, skilled trades with safety regulations, and businesses operating under strict compliance frameworks maintain protection through regulatory barriers that prioritize human accountability.

Location-specific market knowledge provides advantages that cannot be easily replicated through centralized systems. Businesses serving local markets with unique characteristics, regional preferences, or community relationships benefit from proximity and specialized knowledge that distant competitors struggle to match.

To identify additional resilient sectors, examine industries where liability concerns, safety requirements, or regulatory oversight slow technology adoption. Look for businesses where the cost of error is high enough to require human oversight, or where personal trust and relationships drive customer loyalty more than price or convenience.

The Art of "Buying Revenue"

Traditional investors focus on buying undervalued assets. However, a more effective approach involves acquiring predictable revenue streams and implementing systems to scale them efficiently. This shifts the focus from passive market participation to active business development.

Revenue predictability serves as the primary selection criterion. Businesses with subscription models, long-term contracts, or recurring customer relationships provide the stable foundation necessary for growth investments. Consistent revenue patterns allow for confident capital allocation and expansion planning.

Pro forma analysis provides the foundation for acquisition decisions when evaluating scalability potential. Understanding what future cash flows look like under your management may be the difference in closing a deal and walking away. A comprehensive **discounted cash flow** (DCF) analysis using 5-year pro forma projections with terminal value calculations and **weighted average cost of capital** (WACC) provides the most accurate valuation framework.

While **industry multiples** are commonly used for valuing businesses, this approach often fails to capture the true intrinsic value of a business, particularly when significant operational improvements are planned. Pro forma modeling should account for specific operational changes you plan to implement, realistic timelines for improvements, and conservative assumptions about market conditions. This DCF analysis provides the actual basis for determining fair value rather than depending on industry multiples that may not reflect the business's true potential under different management.

Understanding Capital Requirements

Business acquisition requires substantial initial capital, and understanding these requirements helps determine realistic acquisition targets and financing strategies. Most viable service businesses suitable for acquisition require $100,000 to $500,000 in total investment, including down payment, working capital, and initial improvements.

Down payment requirements typically range from 20-30% of the purchase price for established businesses with positive cash flow. SBA loans can reduce this to 10-15% for qualified buyers, but require strong personal credit and industry experience. Seller financing often provides the most flexible terms, particularly when the seller remains involved in transition.

Working capital needs vary by business type but generally require 2-4 months of operating expenses in reserve. Service businesses with monthly recurring revenue need less working capital than those dependent on seasonal or project-based income. Factor these requirements into your total capital planning rather than focusing solely on the purchase price.

Improvement capital should be budgeted for immediate operational enhancements, technology upgrades, and growth investments. Plan for 10-20% of the purchase price in improvement capital during the first year, though specific amounts depend on the business's current operational efficiency and growth potential.

Integration opportunities distinguish sound acquisitions from exceptional ones. Acquiring a business means purchasing both current operations and the potential for operational improvements through technology integration, process automation, and enhanced decision-making systems. The most valuable acquisitions offer clear paths for immediate operational enhancements.

An effective acquisition analysis framework includes:

1. **Current Cash Flow**: Document existing revenue generation and sustainability
2. **Operational Enhancement Potential**: Identify processes suitable for automation or improvement
3. **Market Expansion**: Assess opportunities to serve additional customer segments or markets
4. **Competitive Advantages**: Evaluate how operational improvements create market barriers
5. **Exit Strategy**: Project business valuation following operational enhancements

Building a Business Portfolio

Portfolio construction for scalable businesses focuses on systematic acquisition and management development rather than passive diversification. You're building an operating company that owns multiple businesses, requiring both deal sourcing capabilities and management infrastructure that scales with your acquisitions.

The first acquisition establishes your operational model and management approach. Start with a business you can personally manage while developing systems for operations, financial reporting, and performance monitoring. This initial acquisition serves as your testing ground for scalability improvements and management processes that you'll replicate across future purchases.

Management development pipeline becomes critical as you add businesses to your portfolio. Your role evolves from hands-on operator to deal sourcer and problem solver. Successful managers handle day-to-day operations while you focus on finding the next acquisition and addressing whatever issues arise across your businesses—essentially becoming a "frog kisser," evaluating countless opportunities to find the few worth pursuing.

Geographic and model expansion follows proven operational success. Once you've demonstrated the ability to improve and manage one business profitably, seek similar opportunities in adjacent markets or complementary business models. The goal is leveraging your operational expertise across multiple acquisitions rather than diversifying into unfamiliar territory.

As the portfolio grows, deal flow development becomes your primary focus. Successful business acquisition requires examining numerous opportunities to find suitable targets. Develop relationships with business brokers, industry contacts, and other deal sources. Your time shifts from day-to-day operations to evaluating potential acquisitions, conducting due diligence, and negotiating purchases. This transition from operator to deal sourcer represents the natural evolution of building a scalable business portfolio.

Due Diligence as the Foundation of Success

Thorough due diligence represents the critical difference between successful acquisitions and costly mistakes. While others rely on surface-level financial reviews, comprehensive analysis uncovers the operational realities and growth potential that determine long-term success.

Building your deal team should be your first priority before pursuing any acquisitions. Establish relationships with a qualified attorney experienced in business transactions and a CPA familiar with acquisition analysis. These professionals become your core advisory team, providing expertise you cannot replicate internally. Choose advisors who understand your acquisition strategy and growth objectives rather than those focused solely on minimizing transaction risk.

Also look for professionals who will consider performance-based compensation structures. For example, an attorney willing to accept higher fees for successful transactions and reduced rates for deals that don't close demonstrates alignment with your growth-focused approach. This payment structure indicates they share your commitment to getting deals done rather than simply billing hours regardless of outcomes.

An operational infrastructure assessment examines the business's systems, processes, and organizational capabilities. Are operations documented and standardized? Can management systems handle increased volume without proportional staff increases? Do they have reliable financial reporting and performance measurement systems? Businesses with well-documented, systematized operations scale more effectively than those dependent on individual expertise or informal processes.

Evaluating the management team focuses on operational competence and growth orientation rather than just industry experience. Assess management's ability to implement improvements, adapt to changing market conditions, and execute expansion plans. The most valuable management teams demonstrate track records of operational improvement and strategic thinking beyond maintaining current performance levels.

Financial stress testing models various operational scenarios and their impact on cash flow, profitability, and growth potential. Analyze performance under different market conditions, competitive pressures, and expansion timelines. This analysis reveals the business's resilience and helps identify potential operational improvements that justify the acquisition price.

The Franchise Alternative

Franchising represents another viable path to business ownership, offering structured systems and proven business models that reduce many startup risks. However, franchises should not be considered a shortcut to immediate profitability. Most franchise operations require significant time and capital investment before generating meaningful cash flow, often taking 12-18 months to reach break-even and longer to achieve substantial earnings.

The statistical advantage of franchising over independent business creation is notable. More than 1 in 5 U.S. businesses fail in their first year, according to U.S. Bureau of Labor Statistics data, while the success rate for one year of new franchises is 6.3% higher than independent companies. Studies show that 92% of franchise placements are still in business after two years. This improved success rate stems from established operational systems, brand recognition, and ongoing franchisor support that independent businesses must develop from scratch.

Financing franchise acquisitions often proves more accessible than funding independent ventures. Lenders view established franchise systems as lower-risk investments, and many franchisors have relationships with preferred lenders to facilitate the financing process. When compiled, the average default rate of the top 20 franchises is less than 1%, demonstrating the financial stability that attracts lender support.

While franchising offers improved odds of survival and easier financing, it requires careful evaluation of the specific franchise system, market conditions, and your operational capabilities. The franchisor's support structure, territorial rights, and long-term viability should be thoroughly assessed before committing capital. Franchising can provide a foundation for business ownership, but success still depends on execution, market understanding, and effective management of the operation.

Implementation Timeline and Milestones

Successful scalable business selection requires systematic implementation rather than opportunistic investing. You need a clear timeline and specific milestones to track progress toward your wealth-building goals.

Phase 1: Foundation Building (Months 1-6)

- Identify 5-10 potential acquisition targets or franchise opportunities
- Conduct preliminary due diligence on top candidates
- Develop relationships with business brokers, franchise consultants, and industry contacts
- Create standardized evaluation frameworks for different business types and franchise systems
- Interview CPAs and attorneys to find a good fit

Phase 2: Active Acquisition (Months 7-18)

- Complete detailed due diligence, including operational readiness assessment
- Make an offer on at least one business or submit a franchise application
- Negotiate purchase terms or franchise agreements that align with your objectives
- Close an acquisition franchise agreement to form your portfolio foundation

Phase 3: Optimization and Scale (Months 19-24)

- Implement growth strategies in the business
- Monitor performance metrics and adjust strategies
- Identify additional acquisition opportunities or franchise models/locations
- Prepare for potential expansion

Key Performance Indicators track your progress toward scalable wealth creation:

- Portfolio revenue growth: Target 10-20% annual growth
- Margin expansion: Aim for 5-15% annual gross margin improvement
- Cash flow generation: Achieve and maintain positive operating cash flow
- Operational improvement progress: Track successful growth projects
- Exit opportunities: Monitor valuation multiples and become familiar with exit strategies

Risk Management

Business acquisition carries inherent risks that require ongoing attention and systematic management approaches. Effective risk management distinguishes successful business owners from those who struggle with unforeseen challenges.

Due diligence risk represents the most critical threat to acquisition success. Incomplete financial records, undisclosed liabilities, or overstated performance can devastate acquisition returns. Engage qualified professionals for comprehensive due diligence, including financial audits, legal reviews, and operational assessments. The cost of thorough due diligence is minimal compared to the potential losses from a poorly understood acquisition.

Key person risk affects many service businesses where the owner or key employees maintain critical customer relationships or operational knowledge. Assess the business's dependence on specific individuals and develop transition plans that preserve customer relationships and operational continuity. Consider earn-out structures that keep key personnel involved during transition periods.

Customer concentration risk occurs when a business depends heavily on a small number of customers for revenue. Analyze customer diversity and contract terms to understand revenue stability. Businesses with high customer concentration require different management approaches and may need customer diversification strategies post-acquisition.

Integration risk encompasses the challenges of combining your operational approach with the acquired business's existing systems and culture. Develop clear integration plans that preserve what works while implementing improvements gradually. Rushed integration often disrupts customer relationships and employee performance.

Financing risk includes the challenges of servicing acquisition debt while funding growth initiatives. Structure debt payments to match the business's cash flow patterns and maintain adequate working capital reserves. Consider how debt service requirements will affect your ability to invest in growth and operational improvements.

This overview covers primary acquisition-specific risks, though individual businesses face additional specialized risks. Risk management requires continuous attention and regular reassessment as business conditions change. The goal is not to eliminate all risks but to identify, understand, and manage them effectively while pursuing growth opportunities.

The Transition to Enduring Wealth

The scalable business selection phase of the FIRE Framework represents your transition from market trader to wealth builder. You're no longer dependent on market timing or trading skills—you're building assets that generate wealth independently of market conditions.

Cash flow independence becomes your first major milestone. When your business portfolio generates enough cash flow to cover your living expenses, you've achieved a fundamental shift in your financial position. You're no longer trading time for money or depending on market appreciation for wealth creation.

Compound growth acceleration represents the second phase of wealth building. As your business scales and generate more cash flow, you reinvest these profits into additional scalable businesses. This creates a compounding effect where your wealth grows exponentially rather than linearly.

Market independence forms the ultimate goal of scalable business investing. When your wealth comes from business operations rather than market appreciation, you're protected from market volatility and economic downturns. Your businesses may be affected by economic conditions, but they're not dependent on investor sentiment or market timing.

The intelligence explosion is creating unprecedented opportunities for those who understand how to identify and capitalize on opportunities. While others chase market trends or worry about disruption, you'll be building a portfolio that generates wealth regardless of short-term fluctuations. Your success depends on disciplined execution, thorough due diligence, and patient capital deployment. The businesses you acquire now will form the foundation of your wealth for decades to come, representing investments in proven business models rather than speculative opportunities. Building a scalable business portfolio positions you to benefit from technological advancement while maintaining control over your wealth creation, transforming you from a market participant into a business owner with enduring competitive advantages.

Chapter Nine

Endure: Managing Your Empire

The smartest money doesn't just acquire businesses—it structures them for enduring success. While others struggle with operational chaos and management burnout, you'll be building systematic approaches that allow your businesses to thrive independently of your daily involvement. This chapter shows you how to transform from a business owner who works in the business to one who works on the business, creating sustainable wealth that endures regardless of market conditions or personal circumstances.

The Endurance Advantage

Most new business owners make a critical error: they become the bottleneck in their own success. They handle every decision, manage every relationship, and solve every problem personally. This approach might work for a single, relatively small business, but it becomes impossible when managing multiple acquisitions or scaling operations.

The businesses that endure and generate lasting wealth operate through systems, not personalities. They have documented processes, trained management teams, and operational frameworks that function effectively whether the owner is present or absent. This systematic approach doesn't just improve efficiency—it creates valuable, transferable assets that can be scaled, sold, or passed to the next generation.

Consider the difference between a plumbing company where the owner answers every call and performs every estimate versus one with standardized pricing, trained technicians, and management systems that handle routine operations. The first business dies with its owner; the second becomes a valuable asset that generates wealth for decades.

Building Management Infrastructure

The foundation of enduring business success lies in developing management infrastructure that can operate independently of your direct involvement. This infrastructure includes both human resources and systematic processes that ensure consistent performance across all business operations.

Developing Your Management Team

Your first priority after acquiring any business should be identifying and developing management talent. This doesn't mean hiring expensive executives—it means finding capable people within the organization and giving them the tools, training, and authority they need to manage daily operations effectively.

Start by identifying natural leaders within the existing team. These are often long-term employees who understand the business culture, know the customers, and have earned respect from their peers. While they may lack formal management training, their institutional knowledge and credibility make them valuable management candidates.

Implement a systematic management development program that includes clear job descriptions, performance metrics, and advancement paths. A service technician who consistently receives positive customer feedback and demonstrates leadership qualities might become a crew leader, then a regional supervisor, and eventually a general manager. This progression provides career advancement opportunities while developing the management depth your business needs.

Establish regular management meetings focused on operational performance, problem-solving, and strategic planning. These meetings serve multiple purposes: they keep you informed about business operations, they develop decision-making skills in your management team, and they create accountability for results. Weekly operational reviews and monthly strategic planning sessions create the rhythm necessary for effective business management.

Creating Standard Operating Procedures

Systematic operations require documented procedures that ensure consistent performance regardless of which employee handles specific tasks. These standard operating procedures (SOPs) become the foundation for training new employees, maintaining quality standards, and scaling operations efficiently.

Begin with customer-facing processes that directly impact service quality and customer satisfaction. Document how customer calls are handled, how estimates are prepared, how work is performed, and how follow-up occurs. These procedures should be detailed enough that a new employee can deliver consistent service while flexible enough to handle unique customer situations.

Develop operational checklists for routine tasks that ensure nothing important gets overlooked. A maintenance checklist for service vehicles, a quality control checklist for completed jobs, or a financial reporting checklist for monthly operations all help maintain standards while reducing the mental load on employees and managers.

Create training materials that new employees can use to learn your business systems quickly and effectively. Video training for common procedures, written guides for complex processes, and mentorship programs that pair new employees with experienced team members all accelerate the training process while ensuring consistent knowledge transfer.

Financial Management and Control Systems

Enduring business success requires sophisticated financial management that goes beyond basic bookkeeping. You need systems that provide real-time visibility into business performance, identify potential problems before they become critical, and support informed decision-making across your entire business portfolio.

Performance Monitoring and KPIs

Establish key performance indicators (KPIs) that provide early warning signals about business health and operational efficiency. These metrics should be specific to your industry and business model while remaining simple enough for managers to understand and influence through their daily actions.

Revenue-focused KPIs might include monthly recurring revenue growth, average transaction size, customer acquisition rates, and seasonal performance trends. These metrics help identify market opportunities and potential problems while providing targets for management team performance.

Operational KPIs focus on efficiency and quality metrics that drive customer satisfaction and profitability. Examples might include job completion times, customer callback rates, employee productivity measures, and equipment utilization rates. These metrics help optimize operations while maintaining service quality.

Financial KPIs provide insight into business profitability and cash flow health. Gross margin by service type, accounts receivable aging, cash conversion cycles, and working capital requirements all help maintain financial discipline while supporting growth investments.

Cash Flow Management

Systematic cash flow management becomes even more critical when operating multiple businesses or pursuing aggressive growth strategies. You need visibility into cash flow patterns, predictable forecasting systems, and contingency plans for managing cash flow volatility.

Implement weekly cash flow forecasting that projects receipts and disbursements for the next 13 weeks. This rolling forecast helps identify potential cash flow challenges while providing time to address them through operational adjustments, financing arrangements, or strategic decisions.

Establish cash flow triggers that automatically implement specific responses when cash flow falls below predetermined levels. These might include accelerated collection efforts, delayed capital expenditures, or increased focus on higher-margin services. Having predetermined responses eliminates emotional decision-making during stressful periods.

Create cash flow optimization strategies that improve working capital management without compromising customer relationships. These might include offering discounts for early payment, requiring deposits for large projects, or negotiating better payment terms with suppliers. Small improvements in cash conversion cycles can dramatically improve cash flow stability.

Portfolio-Level Financial Coordination

Managing multiple businesses requires portfolio-level financial coordination that maximizes efficiency while maintaining appropriate separation between entities. This coordination includes shared services, consolidated reporting, and strategic capital allocation across your business portfolio.

Centralize administrative functions that benefit from economies of scale while maintaining operational independence for customer-facing activities. Shared accounting, insurance management, and human resource functions can reduce costs while providing professional expertise that individual businesses couldn't afford independently.

Develop consolidated financial reporting that provides visibility into portfolio performance while maintaining detailed reporting for individual business units. Monthly portfolio reviews should include individual business performance, consolidated cash flow analysis, and strategic planning discussions about resource allocation and growth opportunities.

Implement capital allocation frameworks that prioritize investments based on returns, strategic value, and portfolio balance. A systematic approach to evaluating expansion opportunities, equipment purchases, and acquisition targets ensures optimal use of available capital while maintaining financial discipline.

Operational Excellence and Continuous Improvement

Enduring business success requires commitment to operational excellence that goes beyond meeting minimum standards. You need systematic approaches to continuous improvement that enhance efficiency, quality, and customer satisfaction while reducing costs and operational complexity.

Quality Management Systems

Implement quality management systems that ensure consistent service delivery while identifying opportunities for improvement. These systems should be appropriate for your industry and business size while providing meaningful feedback about performance and customer satisfaction.

Establish customer feedback collection systems that provide regular insights into service quality and customer satisfaction. This might include post-service surveys, annual customer reviews, or systematic follow-up calls. The key is collecting feedback consistently and using it to identify improvement opportunities.

Create internal quality audits that evaluate adherence to standard operating procedures and identify potential problems before they affect customers. Regular audits of work quality, customer service procedures, and administrative processes help maintain standards while providing training opportunities for improvement.

Develop corrective action procedures that address quality problems systematically while preventing recurrence. When problems occur, investigate root causes, implement corrections, update procedures if necessary, and follow up to ensure effectiveness. This systematic approach turns problems into improvement opportunities.

Technology Integration and Automation

Strategic technology integration can dramatically improve operational efficiency while reducing administrative burdens on management teams. The key is selecting technologies that address specific operational challenges while remaining simple enough for employees to adopt effectively.

Customer relationship management (CRM) systems help track customer interactions, manage sales pipelines, and identify service opportunities. A well-implemented CRM system improves customer service while providing valuable data about business performance and growth opportunities.

Scheduling and dispatch systems optimize technician utilization while improving customer service through better appointment management and real-time communication. These systems can reduce administrative overhead while improving operational efficiency and customer satisfaction.

Financial management software automates routine bookkeeping tasks while providing real-time visibility into business performance. Integration between operational systems and financial reporting eliminates manual data entry while ensuring accuracy and timeliness of financial information.

Employee Development and Retention

Your employees represent your most valuable asset for building enduring business success. Developing their skills, maintaining their engagement, and retaining top performers directly impacts operational efficiency, customer satisfaction, and long-term business value.

Create career development paths that provide advancement opportunities while meeting business needs for management and technical expertise. Employees who see clear advancement opportunities are more likely to remain with the company while developing skills that benefit business operations.

Implement performance-based compensation systems that align employee incentives with business objectives. This might include productivity bonuses, customer satisfaction incentives, or profit-sharing programs that reward exceptional performance while encouraging continuous improvement.

Establish training programs that develop both technical skills and business knowledge. Cross-training employees in multiple functions increases operational flexibility while providing career development opportunities. Regular training also helps maintain quality standards while adapting to new technologies and industry changes.

Growth Management and Strategic Planning

Sustainable business growth requires systematic planning and management approaches that maintain operational quality while expanding market reach and service capabilities. The key is balancing growth ambitions with operational capabilities to avoid the common mistake of growing faster than systems can support.

Systematic Growth Planning

Develop growth plans that consider market opportunities, operational capabilities, and financial resources. These plans should include specific milestones, resource requirements, and contingency strategies for managing growth challenges while maintaining service quality.

Market analysis should identify growth opportunities that align with your business strengths and operational capabilities. Geographic expansion, service line additions, or customer segment development all require different approaches and resources. Choose growth strategies that leverage existing advantages while building sustainable competitive positions.

Capacity planning ensures that growth doesn't overwhelm operational systems or compromise service quality. This includes staffing plans, equipment requirements, facility needs, and management capabilities necessary to support planned growth levels. Growing beyond your capacity to deliver quality service can damage customer relationships and business reputation.

Financial planning for growth includes working capital requirements, equipment investments, and cash flow impacts of expansion activities. Many businesses fail during growth phases due to inadequate financial planning rather than lack of market opportunity.

Conservative financial planning with adequate reserves helps navigate growth challenges successfully.

Strategic Partnerships and Alliances

Strategic partnerships can accelerate growth while reducing risks and resource requirements. The key is identifying partnerships that provide genuine value while maintaining operational independence and customer relationships.

Supplier partnerships can improve service capabilities while reducing costs and operational complexity. Preferred vendor relationships, volume discounts, and exclusive territory agreements all provide competitive advantages while improving operational efficiency.

Referral partnerships with complementary businesses can generate new customers while providing value to existing clients. A plumbing company might partner with electricians, HVAC contractors, and general contractors to create mutual referral opportunities that benefit all parties.

Technology partnerships can provide access to advanced capabilities without significant internal investment. Software companies, equipment manufacturers, and service providers often offer partnership programs that provide competitive advantages while reducing implementation risks and costs.

Risk Management and Business Protection

Enduring business success requires comprehensive risk management that protects against operational, financial, and strategic threats. This includes both insurance coverage and operational strategies that minimize exposure while maintaining business flexibility.

Operational Risk Management

Operational risks include key employee departure, equipment failure, supplier problems, and customer concentration. While these risks cannot be eliminated entirely, systematic approaches can minimize their impact while maintaining operational continuity.

Key employee risk requires succession planning and cross-training that reduces dependence on individual employees. Document critical knowledge, cross-train employees in essential functions, and maintain strong relationships with all key personnel to reduce the impact of unexpected departures.

Equipment failure risks can be managed through preventive maintenance programs, equipment redundancy, and service agreements that provide rapid response when problems occur. The cost of comprehensive maintenance and backup systems is minimal compared to the revenue lost during equipment downtime.

Customer concentration risks require ongoing customer development and retention efforts that maintain diverse revenue sources. While large customers provide significant revenue opportunities, excessive dependence on any single customer creates vulnerability that requires careful management.

Financial Risk Management

Financial risks include cash flow volatility, credit exposure, economic downturns, and unexpected expenses. Systematic financial management and conservative planning help navigate these challenges while maintaining operational flexibility.

Maintain adequate cash reserves to handle normal business volatility and unexpected expenses. Cash reserves should cover at least 2-3 months of operating expenses for stable businesses and 4-6 months for seasonal or volatile businesses. These reserves provide operational flexibility while reducing stress during challenging periods.

Establish credit facilities before you need them to provide access to additional capital during growth periods or economic challenges. Banking relationships developed during good times provide valuable resources during difficult periods while ensuring access to necessary capital.

Monitor customer credit and payment patterns to identify potential collection problems before they become critical. Early identification of payment problems allows intervention that often resolves issues while maintaining customer relationships.

Building Legacy Value

The ultimate goal of business ownership extends beyond current income to creating lasting value that can benefit future generations. This requires strategic thinking about business development, succession planning, and wealth preservation that creates enduring value regardless of personal circumstances.

Business Valuation and Value Creation

Understanding what drives business value helps guide operational and strategic decisions that maximize long-term wealth creation. Business value depends on predictable cash flow, growth potential, operational systems, and competitive advantages that can be transferred to new owners.

Document all business systems, procedures, and relationships to create transferable value that doesn't depend on your personal involvement. Well-documented businesses command higher valuations while providing more options for succession planning or eventual sale.

Develop multiple revenue streams and customer relationships that reduce business risk while increasing value. Diversified businesses with multiple service lines, customer segments, and revenue sources typically command premium valuations while providing more stable cash flow.

Create operational systems that can function independently of your direct involvement. Businesses that require constant owner involvement have limited value and few succession options. Systematic operations with capable management teams create valuable assets that generate wealth for decades.

Succession Planning and Exit Strategies

Every business owner should develop succession plans that provide options for transferring business ownership while maximizing value and ensuring operational continuity. These plans should address both planned transitions and unexpected circumstances that require immediate action.

Family succession requires careful planning that balances family relationships with business requirements. Not every family member is suited for business ownership, and forcing unsuitable successors into leadership roles can destroy both family relationships and business value.

Management succession involves developing internal leaders who can eventually purchase or manage the business. Employee stock ownership plans, management buyouts, and gradual ownership transfers all provide succession options while maintaining operational continuity.

Strategic sales to competitors or industry consolidators often provide maximum value while ensuring business continuity. Understanding potential buyers and their strategic objectives helps position your business for eventual sale while maximizing transaction value.

Your path forward involves implementing these management and structural systems across your business portfolio while continuing to identify additional acquisition opportunities. The businesses that endure and create lasting wealth operate through systems rather than personalities, generating consistent returns while building transferable value that creates generational wealth.

The next phase of your wealth-building journey focuses on growing, preserving and protecting the wealth you've created while developing sophisticated strategies for generational wealth transfer and legacy planning. You'll learn how to structure your assets for maximum protection while ensuring your wealth continues growing for decades to come.

You've made it this far, and I hope you're enjoying the book and finding valuable insights. If you have found even one piece of information helpful, your fellow readers would love to hear about it.

Why Your Review Matters:

- Helps others find helpful information
- Guides the development of future books and resources
- Contributes to a community of like-minded readers

Leave Your Review in 60 Seconds: Simply click or scan the QR code below to leave your review on Amazon. It only takes a minute, but your influence could last a lifetime.

Part III: Dominate

RIVANNA HEIGHTS MEDIA

Rivanna Heights Media

Chapter Ten

Managing Your Business Portfolio

Your business portfolio will either become your wealth engine or your wealth trap. The difference lies in how you manage it. Most entrepreneurs who acquire multiple businesses make the fatal mistake of treating each one like their first startup—pouring endless hours into operations, drowning in details, and ultimately creating expensive hobbies instead of wealth-generating assets. This approach transforms what should be your path to financial freedom into an operational nightmare that consumes your time, energy, and sanity.

The truth is that portfolio management requires a fundamentally different mindset than running a single business. You're no longer an operator—you're an orchestrator. Your job isn't to do the work; it's to ensure the work gets done efficiently and profitably without your constant involvement. This shift from hands-on management to strategic oversight is what separates successful wealth builders from exhausted business owners who own jobs instead of assets.

The Management Paradox

Here's what most people don't understand about managing multiple businesses: the more you try to control everything, the less control you actually have. This paradox trips up even experienced entrepreneurs who've built successful companies from the ground up. They assume the same intensive approach that worked for their first business will work for their portfolio. It won't.

When you're managing one business, you can afford to be involved in every decision. You can review every contract, approve every hire, and oversee every major initiative. But when you're managing three, five, or ten businesses, this approach becomes impossible. You become the bottleneck that slows down every operation instead of the catalyst that accelerates growth.

The solution isn't to work harder—it's to work systematically. You need frameworks, processes, and systems that allow you to maintain strategic control while delegating operational control. This requires a complete reimagining of how you approach business ownership.

Building Your Management Foundation

The foundation of successful portfolio management rests on three core principles: delegation without abdication, visibility without micromanagement, and systems without rigidity. These principles guide every decision you make about how to structure your portfolio operations.

Delegation without abdication means you transfer responsibility for execution while maintaining accountability for results. You're not abandoning your businesses—you're empowering others to run them according to your standards and expectations. This requires clear communication of objectives, robust reporting systems, and regular check-ins that focus on outcomes rather than processes.

Visibility without micromanagement ensures you have the information you need to make strategic decisions without getting bogged down in operational details. You need dashboards that show you the health of each business at a glance, but you don't need to know every customer complaint or every employee issue. Your goal is to spot trends, identify opportunities, and catch problems before they become crises.

Systems without rigidity create consistency across your portfolio while allowing each business to adapt to its unique circumstances. You want standardized processes for key functions like financial reporting, performance management, and strategic planning, but you also want the flexibility to modify these systems based on industry requirements or market conditions.

Effectively Managing Without Operational Overwhelm

The first key to managing your portfolio effectively is establishing clear boundaries between strategic and operational responsibilities. You handle strategy; your teams handle operations. This sounds simple, but it requires discipline to maintain these boundaries, especially when operational fires demand your attention.

Start by defining what decisions require your direct involvement and which ones can be made by your management teams. Generally, you should reserve decisions about major capital investments, strategic direction changes, key personnel appointments, and significant policy modifications. Everything else should be delegated to qualified managers who understand your expectations and have the authority to act.

Create a communication rhythm that keeps you informed without overwhelming you with information. This might include weekly dashboard reviews, monthly one-on-one meetings with key managers, and quarterly business reviews that dive deeper into performance and strategy. The key is consistency—your teams need to know when and how they'll communicate with you, and you need to stick to this schedule.

Implement escalation protocols that define when issues should be brought to your attention. Not every problem requires your involvement, but certain types of problems—those involving legal issues, major customer losses, or significant financial impacts—should trigger immediate communication. Your teams should understand these protocols and feel comfortable using them when necessary.

The Art of Strategic Delegation

Effective delegation starts with hiring the right people and ends with holding them accountable for results. But there's a crucial middle step that many portfolio managers skip: clearly defining success and providing the resources necessary to achieve it.

When you delegate responsibility for a business function, you need to specify not just what you want done, but how you'll measure success. This means establishing key performance indicators (KPIs) that align with your overall business objectives. For a sales manager, this might include revenue targets, customer acquisition costs, and retention rates. For an operations manager, it might include efficiency metrics, quality scores, and cost per unit.

But KPIs alone aren't enough. You also need to ensure your managers have the authority, resources, and support they need to achieve these targets. This might mean adjusting budgets, modifying processes, or providing additional training. The goal is to create an environment where success is both expected and achievable.

Regular performance reviews should focus on outcomes rather than activities. You don't need to know how many calls your sales manager made last week; you need to know whether they're on track to hit their quarterly targets. If they're not, your job is to help them identify obstacles and solutions, not to micromanage their daily activities.

Monitoring KPIs for Scalable Growth

The second key to portfolio management is implementing monitoring systems that give you visibility into business performance without requiring constant attention. This means creating dashboards that highlight the most important metrics for each business and alert you to significant changes or trends.

Different businesses require different metrics, but certain KPIs are universal indicators of business health. Revenue growth, profit margins, customer acquisition costs, customer lifetime value, and cash flow are fundamental metrics that apply to almost every business. These should be tracked consistently across your portfolio to enable comparison and benchmarking.

Industry-specific metrics are equally important. A software company might track monthly recurring revenue, churn rates, and user engagement. A manufacturing business might focus on production efficiency, quality metrics, and inventory turnover. A service business might monitor utilization rates, project margins, and client satisfaction scores.

The key is to focus on leading indicators rather than lagging indicators. Revenue is a lagging indicator—it tells you what happened last month. But sales pipeline, customer inquiries, and market share are leading indicators that help you predict what will happen next month. Both types of metrics are important, but leading indicators give you more time to respond to changes.

Create automated reporting systems that deliver this information to you on a regular schedule. Daily reports should focus on critical metrics that require immediate attention. Weekly reports should provide a broader view of business performance. Monthly reports should include trend analysis and strategic insights. Quarterly reports should dive deep into performance drivers and strategic opportunities.

Building Systems for Passive Income Generation

The third key to portfolio management is creating systems that generate income without requiring your constant involvement. This is the ultimate goal of business ownership—building assets that work for you rather than businesses that require you to work for them.

Start by standardizing core processes across your portfolio. This might include financial reporting, human resources management, marketing execution, and customer service delivery. Standardization doesn't mean identical processes—it means consistent approaches that can be managed efficiently across multiple businesses.

Implement technology solutions that automate routine tasks and provide real-time visibility into business operations. Customer relationship management (CRM) systems can automate sales processes and track customer interactions. Enterprise resource planning (ERP) systems can integrate financial, operational, and human resources data. Marketing automation platforms can handle lead generation and customer communication.

But technology alone isn't enough. You also need to create organizational structures that function independently of your involvement. This means developing management layers that can make decisions, solve problems, and drive growth without requiring your input on every issue.

Cross-train key personnel to ensure business continuity and reduce dependence on individual employees. Document critical processes so they can be replicated and improved over time. Create succession plans for key roles so you're not vulnerable to unexpected departures.

Performance Metrics That Matter

Not all metrics are created equal. Some provide valuable insights into business performance, while others are merely interesting data points that don't drive decision-making. The key is focusing on metrics that directly correlate with business success and can be influenced by management action.

Financial metrics form the foundation of business performance measurement. Revenue growth indicates market acceptance and business expansion. Profit margins reflect operational efficiency and pricing power. Cash flow measures the business's ability to generate money and fund operations. Return on investment (ROI) shows how effectively you're using capital to generate returns.

Operational metrics provide insights into business efficiency and effectiveness. Customer acquisition cost (CAC) measures how much you spend to acquire each new customer. Customer lifetime value (CLV) indicates how much revenue each customer generates over their relationship with your business. The ratio of CLV to CAC is a key indicator of business sustainability and profitability.

Strategic metrics help you understand your competitive position and long-term prospects. Market share indicates your position relative to competitors. Customer satisfaction scores predict retention and referral rates. Employee engagement metrics correlate with productivity and retention. Brand awareness measures your marketing effectiveness and market positioning.

Create a balanced scorecard that includes financial, operational, and strategic metrics for each business in your portfolio. This provides a comprehensive view of business performance and helps you identify areas that need attention or investment.

The Technology Stack for Management

Modern portfolio management requires sophisticated technology solutions that provide real-time visibility, automate routine tasks, and enable efficient communication across multiple businesses. Building the right technology stack is essential for managing multiple businesses without becoming overwhelmed by operational details.

Dashboard and reporting tools should provide a unified view of portfolio performance while allowing you to drill down into specific business metrics. These tools should integrate data from multiple sources and present it in easily digestible formats. Look for solutions that offer customizable dashboards, automated alerts, and mobile access.

Communication platforms should enable efficient interaction with your management teams across all businesses. This might include video conferencing tools for regular meetings, project management platforms for tracking initiatives, and messaging systems for quick communication. The key is consistency—using the same platforms across all businesses to streamline communication and reduce complexity.

Financial management systems should provide consolidated reporting across your portfolio while maintaining detailed records for each business. This includes accounting software that can handle multiple entities, budgeting tools that enable comparison across businesses, and cash flow management systems that optimize working capital across your portfolio.

Human resources platforms should standardize key HR processes across your portfolio while accommodating the unique needs of each business. This includes payroll systems, performance management tools, and benefits administration platforms. Standardization reduces administrative overhead and ensures consistent treatment of employees across your portfolio.

Avoiding Common Management Mistakes

Most portfolio managers make predictable mistakes that reduce returns and increase operational complexity. Understanding these mistakes and how to avoid them is crucial for building a successful portfolio management practice.

The micromanagement trap occurs when portfolio managers try to maintain the same level of control they had when managing a single business. This leads to decision bottlenecks, frustrated managers, and reduced operational efficiency. The solution is to clearly define decision-making authority and stick to strategic oversight rather than operational involvement.

The dashboard overload mistake happens when managers try to track too many metrics across too many businesses. This creates information overload and makes it difficult to focus on what really matters. The solution is to focus on a small number of key metrics that directly correlate with business success and portfolio value.

The inconsistent communication error occurs when managers don't establish regular communication rhythms with their business teams. This leads to surprises, missed opportunities, and deteriorating relationships. The solution is to create consistent communication schedules and stick to them regardless of how busy you become.

The resource allocation blunder happens when managers don't properly allocate capital and management attention across their portfolio. This often results in over-investing in struggling businesses while under-investing in high-potential opportunities. The solution is to regularly evaluate resource allocation and make adjustments based on performance and potential.

Building Your Management Team

As your portfolio grows, you'll need to build a team of professionals who can help you manage the complexity and scale your operations. This team should include both internal resources and external advisors who bring specialized expertise to your portfolio.

Internal team members might include a portfolio manager who oversees day-to-day operations, a financial analyst who monitors performance and prepares reports, and an operations coordinator who ensures consistent implementation of processes across businesses. The size and composition of your internal team will depend on the size and complexity of your portfolio.

External advisors should include professionals who provide specialized expertise that you don't have internally. This might include accountants who handle tax planning and compliance, lawyers who manage legal issues and structures, and consultants who provide industry-specific expertise. The key is building relationships with trusted advisors who understand your portfolio and can provide strategic guidance.

Business-specific management should include qualified managers who can run each business independently while meeting your performance expectations. These managers should have both the technical skills required for their industry and the leadership skills necessary to manage teams and drive results.

Creating Value Through Synergies

One of the biggest advantages of portfolio management is the ability to create value through synergies between businesses. These synergies can reduce costs, increase revenues, and improve competitive positioning across your portfolio.

Cost synergies occur when businesses can share resources or processes to reduce overall expenses. This might include consolidated purchasing power, shared administrative functions, or common technology platforms. The key is identifying opportunities for cost reduction without compromising business performance.

Revenue synergies happen when businesses can cross-sell products or services, share customer bases, or combine capabilities to create new offerings. These synergies often provide the highest returns but require careful coordination to execute effectively.

Knowledge synergies emerge when businesses can share expertise, best practices, or market insights. This might include sharing successful marketing strategies, operational improvements, or strategic insights that help other businesses in your portfolio perform better.

Financial synergies can occur through more efficient capital allocation, improved financing terms, or better risk management across your portfolio. This might include using cash flow from stable businesses to fund growth in high-potential businesses or leveraging the combined portfolio to negotiate better financing terms.

Scaling Your Management Approach

As your portfolio grows, your management approach must evolve to handle increased complexity and scale. This requires systematically upgrading your processes, systems, and team to maintain efficiency and effectiveness.

Process standardization becomes increasingly important as you add more businesses to your portfolio. This means creating templates, checklists, and procedures that can be applied consistently across different businesses while accommodating their unique requirements.

System integration ensures that information flows efficiently between businesses and up to your portfolio management level. This might require upgrading technology platforms, implementing new reporting systems, or creating data warehouses that consolidate information from multiple sources.

Team development involves building the capabilities of your management team to handle increased responsibility and complexity. This includes training, coaching, and potentially adding new team members with specialized skills.

Culture alignment ensures that all businesses in your portfolio operate according to your values and standards while maintaining their unique characteristics. This requires clear communication of expectations, regular reinforcement of key messages, and consistent recognition of behaviors that align with your culture.

Preparing for the Next Level

Business management is a skill that improves with practice and experience. As you become more comfortable managing multiple businesses, you'll identify new opportunities to optimize performance, reduce risk, and create value. The key is maintaining a learning mindset and continuously improving your approach.

Stay connected with other portfolio managers and business owners who can share insights and best practices. Join industry associations, attend conferences, and participate in peer groups that focus on portfolio management and business ownership.

Regularly evaluate your portfolio composition and consider whether changes are needed. This might mean selling businesses that no longer fit your strategy, acquiring new businesses that complement your existing portfolio, or restructuring businesses to improve their performance.

The strategies and systems you develop for managing your business portfolio will serve as the foundation for the next phase of your wealth-building journey. With a well-managed portfolio generating consistent returns and requiring minimal operational involvement, you'll have the financial resources and time flexibility to focus on wealth preservation and strategic growth opportunities.

Chapter Eleven

Wealth Preservation Structures

Protecting your wealth requires more than just earning it. The moment you accumulate significant assets from your AI-driven investments, you enter a new battlefield where taxes, lawsuits, and regulatory changes can destroy decades of hard work overnight. Without proper protection structures, even the most successful wealth extraction becomes vulnerable to forces beyond your control.

Most entrepreneurs who profit from the intelligence explosion make a fatal error: they focus exclusively on making money while ignoring the equally critical task of keeping it. They build impressive portfolios but leave them exposed to predators who view successful investors as walking ATMs. This chapter will show you how to build an impenetrable fortress around your AI-generated wealth.

Your financial future depends on understanding that wealth preservation isn't optional—it's the foundation that determines whether your success lasts one generation or ten.

The Three-Layer Defense System

Building unbreakable wealth protection requires a strategic approach that addresses every potential threat. Think of your wealth as a castle that needs multiple layers of defense. The outer walls protect against common attacks, the inner walls guard against sophisticated threats, and the keep itself shields your most valuable assets from complete destruction.

This three-layer system addresses the reality that wealth faces different types of risks at different stages. Early-stage protection focuses on basic asset separation and tax optimization. Mid-stage protection adds sophisticated legal structures and jurisdictional advantages. Advanced protection creates generational wealth transfer mechanisms that outlast economic cycles and regulatory changes.

Each layer builds upon the previous one, creating redundancy that ensures your wealth survives even if one defense fails. This approach has protected generational wealth for centuries, and it's exactly what you need to secure your AI-generated profits.

Layer One: Legal Structures for Tax Optimization and Asset Protection

The foundation of wealth preservation starts with creating proper legal structures that separate your assets from personal liability while minimizing your tax burden. These structures serve as the first line of defense against creditors, lawsuits, and excessive taxation that can drain your wealth faster than you can rebuild it.

Limited Liability Companies (LLCs) for Asset Separation

LLCs provide the most flexible foundation for protecting your AI-generated wealth. Unlike corporations, LLCs offer pass-through taxation while maintaining strong liability protection. This means your business profits flow directly to your personal tax return, avoiding double taxation while keeping your assets separate from personal creditors.

The key to effective LLC protection lies in proper setup and maintenance. You'll need separate LLCs for different types of assets—one for your trading activities, another for real estate investments, and possibly a third for business acquisitions. This separation prevents creditors from attacking one LLC and gaining access to assets held in others.

Each LLC must maintain proper documentation, separate bank accounts, and formal operating agreements. Courts can pierce the corporate veil if you treat LLCs as extensions of your personal finances. This means no commingling of funds, no personal expenses paid from business accounts, and regular meetings documented with formal minutes.

Domestic Asset Protection Trusts (DAPTs)

Several states now offer domestic asset protection trusts that provide significant creditor protection while keeping your assets within the United States. Delaware, Nevada, and South Dakota lead this space with strong debtor-friendly laws and experienced trust administration.

DAPTs allow you to be a discretionary beneficiary of your own trust while maintaining significant creditor protection. This means you can potentially access trust assets for your benefit while making it extremely difficult for creditors to reach those same assets. The trust's independent trustee provides the legal separation necessary for protection.

The strongest DAPTs include spendthrift clauses that prevent creditors from attaching trust assets, even if you're a beneficiary. They also feature short statute of limitations periods that quickly cut off creditor claims. Nevada's two-year statute of limitations means creditors must act quickly or lose their ability to attack trust assets entirely.

Offshore Structures for Maximum Protection

For high-net-worth individuals with significant AI-generated wealth, offshore structures provide the ultimate level of asset protection. Countries like the Cook Islands, Nevis, and Belize offer legal systems specifically designed to protect assets from foreign creditors and judgments.

Offshore trusts work by moving your assets outside the jurisdiction of U.S. courts. Even if a creditor obtains a judgment against you, enforcing that judgment in a protective jurisdiction becomes extremely difficult and expensive. Most creditors will settle for pennies on the dollar rather than pursue expensive international litigation.

The Cook Islands Asset Protection Trust (CIAPT) represents the gold standard in offshore protection. Cook Islands law requires creditors to prove their case beyond a reasonable doubt—a criminal standard that's nearly impossible to meet in civil litigation. The trust also includes a "flee clause" that automatically moves assets to another jurisdiction if the current one becomes compromised.

Tax Optimization Strategies

Proper wealth preservation structures can significantly reduce your tax burden while maintaining full legal compliance. The key lies in understanding how different entities and jurisdictions treat various types of income and gains.

Strategy	Tax Benefit	Protection Level	Complexity
Single-Member LLC	Pass-through taxation	Moderate	Low
Multi-Member LLC	Partnership taxation	High	Medium
S-Corporation	No self-employment tax on distributions	Moderate	Medium
C-Corporation	21% corporate tax rate	High	High
Domestic Trust	Grantor trust benefits	High	Medium
Offshore Trust	Potential tax deferral	Maximum	High

Delaware Statutory Trusts (DSTs) offer unique tax advantages for real estate investments. These trusts allow you to defer capital gains taxes through 1031 exchanges while maintaining professional management and fractional ownership. This structure works particularly well for reinvesting trading profits into income-producing real estate.

Captive Insurance Companies

High-income earners can create captive insurance companies to self-insure against various risks while generating significant tax deductions. These companies can insure everything from business interruption to key person life insurance, creating legitimate business expenses that reduce taxable income.

Captive insurance companies must meet strict IRS requirements to maintain their tax-advantaged status. They need real insurance risks, arm's length transactions, and proper capitalization. When structured correctly, they can provide annual tax deductions of up to $2.3 million while building tax-deferred wealth inside the insurance company.

Layer Two: Intergenerational Wealth Transfer Systems

Building wealth that lasts beyond your lifetime requires sophisticated planning that addresses gift taxes, estate taxes, and generation-skipping transfer taxes. These systems ensure your AI-generated wealth benefits your children and grandchildren rather than government coffers.

Grantor Retained Annuity Trusts (GRATs)

GRATs allow you to transfer future appreciation to your heirs while retaining the current value of your assets. This strategy works particularly well with volatile AI-related investments that have high growth potential but uncertain timing.

Here's how GRATs work: You transfer assets to a trust that pays you a fixed annuity for a specific term. If the assets appreciate beyond the IRS's assumed interest rate (known as the 7520 rate), the excess growth passes to your beneficiaries gift-tax-free. If the assets don't appreciate, they simply return to you at the end of the term.

Rolling GRATs provide even more powerful wealth transfer opportunities. Instead of creating one long-term GRAT, you create a series of shorter-term GRATs that roll over every two years. This approach captures growth during up markets while limiting risk during down markets.

Charitable Remainder Trusts (CRTs)

CRTs offer a unique combination of tax benefits, income generation, and wealth transfer opportunities. You contribute appreciated assets to the trust, receive an immediate tax deduction, and get income payments for life or a specified term. Whatever remains in the trust at the end goes to charity.

The key advantage of CRTs lies in their ability to sell appreciated assets without immediate capital gains taxation. If you have significant gains from your AI investments, contributing them to a CRT allows the trust to sell and reinvest the full proceeds. You'll receive income based on the entire amount rather than the after-tax proceeds.

CRTs can be structured as charitable remainder annuity trusts (CRATs) that pay fixed dollar amounts, or charitable remainder unitrusts (CRUTs) that pay fixed percentages of trust value. CRUTs offer inflation protection and participate in trust growth, while CRATs provide predictable income streams.

Generation-Skipping Transfer Tax Planning

The generation-skipping transfer (GST) tax imposes a 40% penalty on transfers to grandchildren and more remote descendants. However, proper planning can use your $12.92 million GST exemption (as of 2023) to create dynasty trusts that benefit multiple generations tax-free.

Dynasty trusts can last for hundreds of years in states with favorable perpetuity laws. These trusts hold assets for the benefit of all your descendants, providing distributions for education, health, and other needs while preserving principal for future generations. The key is allocating GST exemption to these trusts when you fund them, protecting all future growth from transfer taxes.

Family Limited Partnerships (FLPs)

FLPs provide powerful valuation discounts that can significantly reduce gift and estate taxes. You contribute assets to a partnership, retain a small general partner interest for control, and gift limited partner interests to family members over time.

The limited partner interests qualify for discounts due to lack of control and marketability. These discounts typically range from 20% to 40%, meaning you can transfer $1 million of underlying assets by using only $600,000 to $800,000 of gift tax exemption. Over time, these discounts compound to transfer significant wealth tax-efficiently.

Installment Sales to Grantor Trusts

This advanced strategy allows you to sell assets to a trust you've created for your family's benefit while receiving installment payments over time. The trust must be structured as a grantor trust, meaning you pay its income taxes, which provides additional tax-free benefits to your heirs.

The installment sale removes all future appreciation from your estate while providing ongoing income. The trust pays you a fixed interest rate (usually the minimum rate required by the IRS), and any growth beyond that rate benefits your heirs. Meanwhile, your payment of the trust's income taxes provides additional tax-free gifts to your beneficiaries.

Layer Three: Protection Against Economic and Regulatory Disruption

The final layer of wealth preservation focuses on protecting your assets from systemic risks that could affect entire asset classes or jurisdictions. These risks include currency devaluation, regulatory changes, and economic disruptions that can't be addressed through traditional legal structures alone.

Geographic Diversification

Spreading your assets across multiple jurisdictions provides protection against country-specific risks. This doesn't mean moving everything offshore—it means strategically positioning assets in stable jurisdictions that complement your primary residence.

Physical precious metals stored in secure facilities outside your home country provide protection against currency devaluation and extreme economic scenarios. Countries like Switzerland, Singapore, and New Zealand offer political stability and strong property rights that can preserve wealth during turbulent times.

Real estate in stable foreign markets provides both geographic diversification and inflation protection. Countries with strong rule of law, growing economies, and favorable exchange rates can offer better long-term returns than domestic markets while providing currency hedging benefits.

Regulatory Hedging Strategies

Governments facing fiscal pressure often target wealthy individuals with new taxes and regulations. Protecting against these risks requires structures that can adapt to changing legal environments while maintaining effectiveness.

Multiple citizenship provides the ultimate regulatory hedge. Countries like Portugal, Malta, and several Caribbean nations offer citizenship-by-investment programs that provide alternative tax residency options. Having multiple passports gives you flexibility to relocate if your primary country becomes hostile to wealth preservation.

Pre-immigration planning allows you to restructure your affairs before moving to a new jurisdiction. This might involve creating offshore trusts, selling appreciated assets, or restructuring business entities to minimize tax impact in your new country of residence.

Crisis-Proof Asset Allocation

Traditional asset allocation models assume normal market conditions and government stability. Protecting generational wealth requires considering extreme scenarios that could devastate conventional portfolios.

The 5-10-15 rule provides a framework for crisis-proof allocation: 5% in physical precious metals, 10% in foreign real estate, and 15% in assets outside your home country's jurisdiction. This allocation provides protection against currency collapse, political instability, and extreme market volatility.

Alternative Investment Vehicles

Private equity, hedge funds, and other alternative investments often provide better protection against inflation and market volatility than traditional assets. These investments also offer structural advantages that can enhance overall portfolio resilience.

Master limited partnerships (MLPs) in energy infrastructure provide tax-advantaged income and inflation protection. These partnerships own assets like pipelines and storage facilities that generate relatively stable cash flows regardless of commodity price volatility.

Real estate investment trusts (REITs) focused on essential properties—medical facilities, utilities, and food distribution—provide income and growth potential while serving basic human needs that remain stable during economic disruptions.

Digital Asset Integration

Cryptocurrency and digital assets represent a new frontier in wealth preservation. While volatile, these assets offer unique advantages including portability, divisibility, and independence from traditional financial systems.

Cold storage wallets kept in multiple secure locations provide protection against both cyber attacks and government seizure. Hardware wallets stored in safe deposit boxes or secure facilities give you control over your digital assets without relying on exchanges or custodians.

Multi-signature wallets require multiple private keys to access funds, providing protection against single points of failure. This approach works particularly well for family wealth, where multiple family members can hold keys that must work together to access assets.

Implementation Timeline and Maintenance

Implementing comprehensive wealth preservation structures requires careful planning and professional coordination. The complexity of these systems means you can't handle implementation alone—you need a team of specialists working together under your direction.

Phase One: Foundation Building (Years 1-3)

Start with basic legal structures that provide immediate protection and tax benefits. This includes creating LLCs for different asset classes, establishing basic trusts, and implementing tax optimization strategies. These foundational elements provide immediate benefits while laying groundwork for more sophisticated planning.

Phase Two: Advanced Protection (Years 2 and on)

Add sophisticated asset protection and tax planning structures. This phase includes offshore trusts, captive insurance companies, and advanced estate planning vehicles. These structures require more time and coordination but provide significantly enhanced protection.

Phase Three: Optimization and Maintenance (Ongoing)

Wealth preservation structures require ongoing maintenance and optimization. Laws change, family circumstances change, and your wealth level changes. Regular reviews ensure your structures remain effective and compliant with current regulations.

Annual reviews should assess structure effectiveness, tax efficiency, and family needs. Market changes might require rebalancing asset allocations or adjusting protection strategies. Regulatory changes might necessitate structural modifications or additional planning techniques.

Professional Team Coordination

Effective wealth preservation requires coordination between multiple professionals including estate planning attorneys, tax advisors, financial planners, and trust officers. Each professional brings specialized expertise, but you need someone to coordinate their efforts and ensure all strategies work together effectively.

Your wealth preservation team should include:

- Estate planning attorney specializing in high-net-worth clients
- Tax advisor with experience in complex structures
- Financial advisor focused on alternative investments
- Trust officer or family office executive
- International tax specialist for offshore structures

Measuring Success and Adjusting Strategies

Effective wealth preservation requires metrics that go beyond simple asset growth. You need to measure protection effectiveness, tax efficiency, and family satisfaction with the structures you've created.

Key Performance Indicators

Track your effective tax rate across all structures and jurisdictions. This metric shows whether your tax optimization strategies are working and identifies areas for improvement. Your goal should be minimizing total taxes while maintaining full legal compliance.

Monitor asset protection effectiveness by tracking legal challenges, creditor claims, and regulatory changes affecting your structures. While you hope never to need these protections, knowing they work provides peace of mind and validates your investment in these systems.

Family Satisfaction Metrics

Wealth preservation isn't just about protecting assets—it's about ensuring your family benefits from your success. Track family member satisfaction with trust distributions, involvement in family wealth decisions, and understanding of wealth preservation principles.

Regular family meetings help ensure everyone understands the structures you've created and their role in maintaining family wealth. These meetings also provide opportunities to adjust strategies based on changing family needs and circumstances.

Your wealth preservation structures should enable your family to thrive while protecting against threats that could destroy everything you've built. The intelligence explosion creates unprecedented opportunities for wealth creation, but it also creates new risks that require sophisticated protection strategies.

The next chapter will show you how to scale these preservation strategies as your wealth grows, ensuring your protection systems remain effective regardless of how much your AI-generated wealth expands. We'll explore advanced techniques for managing multiple structures, coordinating international planning, and building the infrastructure needed to support generational wealth that lasts centuries rather than decades.

Chapter Twelve

Scaling Your Business Empire

Your business empire's true wealth potential lies dormant until you unlock scalable growth. Most entrepreneurs hit a wall when scaling their acquired businesses, adding complexity instead of creating multiplication. They hire more people, implement more systems, and find themselves trapped in operational chaos rather than building the wealth-generating machine they envisioned. The capital you've accumulated from riding the intelligence bubble now faces its ultimate test: can you transform it into sustainable wealth through business empire building?

This chapter transforms you from a business collector into a wealth architect who orchestrates exponential growth without sacrificing the management foundation you've already established.

The Empire Builder's Mindset Shift

Before you can scale effectively, you must abandon the traditional mindset that equates growth with complexity. The capital windfall from your market success gives you a unique advantage—you can acquire businesses and scale them without the financial constraints that limit most entrepreneurs. But this advantage becomes a liability if you approach scaling with the same speculation mindset that generated your initial wealth.

Empire building requires patience, systematic thinking, and operational excellence rather than the rapid decision-making and risk tolerance that characterize successful market speculation. Your businesses must generate consistent returns for decades, not just capitalize on temporary market inefficiencies or technological disruptions.

The empire builder's mindset operates on compound scalability principles where each improvement makes subsequent improvements easier and more effective. This isn't about riding trends or timing markets—it's about building businesses that become more valuable and more profitable as they grow larger.

Revenue Per Complexity Analysis

The foundation of intelligent scaling rests on a crucial metric that most entrepreneurs ignore: Revenue Per Complexity Unit. Every business decision should be measured by how much additional revenue it generates per unit of complexity added. If a new initiative doesn't dramatically improve this ratio, it's not worth pursuing regardless of how profitable it appears on paper.

Calculate this metric for each major business process by dividing annual revenue generated by the total complexity score of people involved, process steps required, and decision points created. This reveals which areas of your business represent scaling sweet spots and which areas are complexity drains that will sabotage your growth efforts.

Service businesses often scale poorly because they require proportional increases in skilled labor as revenue grows. Manufacturing businesses can scale more effectively because fixed costs get distributed across larger production volumes. Understanding these fundamental scaling characteristics helps you focus expansion efforts where they'll generate the highest returns.

Geographic Expansion Strategy

The most straightforward path to scaling involves expanding successful business models into new geographic markets. This approach leverages your existing operational knowledge while accessing new customer bases and revenue streams.

Market similarity analysis helps you identify expansion targets that minimize execution risk. Markets with similar demographics, regulatory environments, and competitive landscapes allow you to replicate successful strategies with minimal modification. This reduces the trial-and-error costs that often derail expansion efforts.

Phased expansion prevents overextension while building expansion capabilities systematically. Start with adjacent markets that share borders or similar characteristics with your existing operations. Success in these markets provides the experience and cash flow needed to tackle more distant or challenging expansion targets.

Local partnership strategies can accelerate expansion while reducing capital requirements and operational complexity. Instead of building everything from scratch, identify established local operators who can implement your systems and processes in exchange for partnership arrangements or acquisition opportunities.

Operational Leverage Through Systematization

The businesses that scale most successfully operate like franchises even when they're not franchises. This means creating systems so robust and comprehensive that new locations or divisions can achieve consistent results without requiring your direct oversight.

Process documentation becomes the foundation of scalable operations. Every critical business function should have detailed procedures that specify exactly how work gets done, what standards must be met, and how problems should be handled. This documentation enables consistent execution across multiple locations and management teams.

Training program development ensures that new employees and managers can quickly achieve competency in your business systems. Standardized training reduces the time and cost required to bring new team members up to speed while ensuring consistent service quality across your empire.

Quality control systems provide early warning when standards begin to slip at any location. Regular audits, customer feedback monitoring, and performance tracking help you maintain consistency as your business grows larger and more geographically dispersed.

The Acquisition Integration Model

Your capital advantage allows you to grow through acquisition rather than just organic expansion. But successful acquisition integration requires systematic approaches that preserve the value you're purchasing while implementing improvements that justify your investment.

Cultural integration planning begins before acquisition closes. Understanding the existing culture, identifying which elements to preserve, and determining how to blend your management philosophy with local practices prevents the cultural disruption that destroys acquisition value.

Systems integration should happen gradually rather than immediately. Dramatic changes often trigger employee departures and customer defections that reduce the business value you've purchased. Phased integration allows you to implement improvements while maintaining operational stability.

Synergy realization focuses on concrete benefits rather than theoretical possibilities. Cross-selling opportunities, shared vendor relationships, and combined purchasing power provide measurable returns that justify acquisition costs. Avoid complex integration schemes that sound good in theory but prove difficult to execute in practice.

Market Position Strengthening

Scaling creates opportunities to strengthen your competitive position in ways that smaller businesses can't achieve. Size advantages, when properly leveraged, create sustainable competitive moats that protect your market position and pricing power.

Market share concentration in specific geographic regions or customer segments creates pricing power and reduces competitive pressure. Instead of spreading thinly across many markets, focus on achieving dominant positions in select markets where you can control competitive dynamics.

Vendor relationship leverage improves as your purchasing volume increases. Larger orders generate better pricing, priority treatment, and customized solutions that smaller competitors can't access. These advantages compound over time as vendor relationships deepen and become more strategically valuable.

Customer relationship depth increases when you can offer comprehensive solutions rather than point services. Businesses that serve multiple customer needs become more valuable to their clients and more difficult for competitors to displace. This relationship depth translates into higher customer lifetime values and more predictable revenue streams.

Capital Allocation Across the Empire

Your financial resources allow you to optimize capital allocation across your business portfolio in ways that maximize overall returns rather than treating each business as an independent entity. This portfolio approach creates significant advantages over competitors who must fund growth from individual business cash flows.

Cross-subsidization strategies enable you to invest in high-potential opportunities while maintaining stable operations in mature businesses. Cash flow from established businesses can fund expansion or improvement initiatives in growth-stage businesses without requiring external financing or diluting ownership.

Resource pooling reduces overall capital requirements while improving resource utilization across your empire. Expensive equipment, specialized expertise, and infrastructure investments can serve multiple businesses, reducing per-unit costs and improving return on investment.

Strategic timing of investments allows you to capitalize on market cycles and competitive opportunities that cash-constrained competitors must pass up. Having available capital when opportunities arise provides significant strategic advantages in acquisition negotiations and market expansion initiatives.

Scaling Through Standardization

The businesses that scale most effectively develop standard operating procedures that work consistently across different locations, markets, and business cycles. This standardization creates predictable outcomes while reducing the management attention required for each location.

Service delivery standardization ensures consistent customer experiences regardless of location or staff changes. Customers should receive the same quality of service whether they're dealing with your newest location or your most established operation. This consistency builds brand value and customer loyalty that supports premium pricing.

Financial management standardization provides visibility into performance across your entire empire while ensuring consistent accounting practices and financial controls. Standardized reporting enables you to identify problems early and share successful practices across all locations.

Hiring and training standardization ensures that you can rapidly scale your workforce while maintaining quality standards. Standardized job descriptions, interview processes, and training programs enable consistent talent acquisition and development across your empire.

Long-Term Value Creation

Building a scalable business empire requires thinking beyond immediate returns to focus on long-term value creation. The businesses you build today should remain valuable and profitable for decades, providing sustainable wealth that survives economic cycles and competitive pressures.

Market positioning for sustainability involves choosing business models and competitive strategies that remain viable even as markets evolve. Businesses built around fundamental human needs or essential services tend to maintain their value better than those dependent on specific technologies or trends.

Operational excellence development creates businesses that continuously improve their efficiency and effectiveness. Companies that systematically reduce costs while improving service quality build sustainable competitive advantages that compound over time.

Leadership development ensures that your businesses can continue performing even as your direct involvement decreases. Building management teams that can operate independently while maintaining your standards and values creates truly scalable assets rather than extensions of your personal capabilities.

The Wealth Preservation Transition

Successfully scaling your business empire creates the foundation for the next phase of your wealth journey. Businesses that generate consistent returns without requiring your operational involvement provide the passive income and asset diversification that support long-term wealth preservation strategies.

The systematic approach to empire scaling transforms your initial market gains into sustainable business assets that continue producing returns regardless of market conditions. As you implement these scaling strategies, you're building the operational foundation that will support your family's wealth for generations.

Your empire scaling decisions today determine whether your market success becomes temporary speculation profits or permanent generational wealth. By focusing on systematic scaling rather than opportunistic expansion, you're transforming capital into assets that will continue appreciating long after the current market cycle ends.

CHAPTER THIRTEEN

STRATEGIC EXIT PLANNING

THE GREATEST WEALTH BUILDERS know when to harvest their gains. You've spent years building and scaling your business empire, transforming market capital into operational assets that generate consistent returns. Now comes the moment that separates true wealth builders from asset collectors—knowing exactly when and how to exit your investments for maximum returns. This chapter reveals the sophisticated strategies that transform good business investments into generational wealth.

The Psychology of Strategic Exits

Most business owners fail at exits because they think like collectors instead of strategists. They fall in love with their businesses, hold too long, and watch peak valuations slip away. You won't make that mistake because you understand the fundamental difference between building wealth and building monuments to your ego.

The Collector's Trap affects even sophisticated entrepreneurs. They build profitable businesses, acquire additional operations, and then simply hold everything forever. They confuse ownership with wealth building, treating their businesses like trophies rather than assets designed to maximize financial returns.

Real wealth builders understand that business ownership is temporary—a vehicle for capturing maximum value before moving to the next opportunity. This mindset shift changes everything about how you evaluate, manage, and time your business exits. From the day you acquire or build a business, you're not just creating operational value; you're creating a future exit opportunity that will fund your next wealth-building cycle.

Consider the strategic difference: A collector buys a business and thinks, "I'll hold this forever and pass it to my children." A strategist acquires the same business and thinks, "I'll maximize this operation for five to seven years, then sell at peak valuation to fund my next three acquisitions." Both approaches can create wealth, but only one creates compound wealth that multiplies across generations.

Market Timing Mastery for Peak Exits

Economic cycle recognition forms the foundation of strategic exit timing. Business valuations move in predictable cycles that correlate with broader economic conditions, industry trends, and capital market dynamics. Understanding these cycles enables you to position your exits during peak valuation periods rather than being forced to sell during market downturns.

Business valuation cycles follow distinct patterns that smart empire builders learn to recognize and exploit. During economic expansion periods, buyers pay premium multiples for stable, growing businesses. Strategic acquirers become more aggressive in their expansion plans, while financial buyers have abundant capital to deploy. These conditions create competitive bidding environments that maximize exit valuations.

Conversely, during economic uncertainty or contraction, buyers become conservative and valuations compress. Strategic acquirers pause expansion plans to focus on internal operations, while financial buyers struggle to secure acquisition financing. Understanding these patterns allows you to time your exits for maximum value capture rather than being forced to accept discounted valuations.

Market sentiment indicators provide early warning signals for optimal exit timing. When business acquisition stories dominate financial media, when similar businesses sell for premiums above historical multiples, and when multiple parties compete aggressively for quality assets, you're likely approaching peak selling conditions. These indicators don't guarantee perfect timing, but they signal when market conditions favor sellers over buyers.

Reading Valuation Multiples Like a Professional

Understanding industry-specific multiples becomes crucial for timing your exits and negotiating maximum value. Different business sectors command different valuations based on their growth prospects, cash flow predictability, and market dynamics. Manufacturing businesses typically trade at lower multiples than service businesses, while technology-enabled operations often command premium valuations.

Traditional multiple benchmarks provide starting points for valuation discussions, but sophisticated exit planning requires understanding the factors that drive premium valuations. Businesses with recurring revenue streams command higher multiples than those dependent on one-time transactions. Operations with strong management teams that can operate independently attract buyers willing to pay acquisition premiums.

Revenue multiple analysis becomes especially important for growing businesses with strong cash flow characteristics. Predictable monthly recurring revenue can command significant valuation premiums because buyers can forecast future performance with greater confidence. Businesses that have systematically reduced customer concentration risks and built diversified revenue streams often achieve valuation multiples that exceed industry averages.

Strategic buyer premiums can add substantial value above financial buyer offers because strategic acquirers value synergies that pure financial buyers cannot capture. When your business complements a buyer's existing operations, provides access to new markets, or eliminates competitive threats, strategic buyers often justify premium valuations that reflect these additional benefits.

The Art of Market Condition Analysis

Macroeconomic indicators signal optimal exit windows that sophisticated wealth builders learn to recognize and exploit. Interest rate environments significantly impact business valuations because they affect the cost of acquisition financing. When rates are low, buyers can finance acquisitions cheaply, driving up the prices they're willing to pay. When rates rise, acquisition financing becomes expensive, compressing the multiples buyers can justify.

Capital market conditions provide additional insight into buyer behavior and valuation trends. High levels of initial public offering activity indicate strong appetite for growth businesses and aggressive valuation environments. When private equity firms have substantial capital to deploy, competition for quality businesses intensifies, driving up acquisition prices.

Industry-specific momentum creates sector rotation effects that impact exit timing for businesses in different markets. Periods of strong investor interest in particular sectors create temporary valuation premiums that savvy empire builders can exploit through well-timed exits. Understanding these momentum shifts allows you to position exits when your specific industry sector commands peak investor attention.

Regulatory environment changes can dramatically impact business valuations, creating both opportunities and threats for strategic exits. Anticipated regulatory changes that might restrict business operations or increase compliance costs often depress valuations, while regulatory changes that create barriers to new competition can increase existing business values.

Advanced Exit Structuring Strategies

The installment sale strategy maximizes after-tax proceeds while managing the risks inherent in any business transition. Rather than receiving all sale proceeds immediately, installment structures spread payments over multiple years, providing tax deferral benefits while ensuring the business performs as expected under new ownership.

Installment sales work particularly well when buyers and sellers have different perspectives on future business performance. Sellers who are confident in their business fundamentals can accept deferred payments in exchange for higher total valuations, while buyers reduce their upfront capital requirements and share performance risks with sellers.

Implementation requires careful attention to payment security and performance milestones. Sellers should require personal guarantees or collateral for deferred payments, while buyers need assurance that business performance metrics are clearly defined and fairly measured. The most successful installment structures include provisions that protect both parties' interests throughout the payment period.

The earn-out structure bridges valuation gaps while maximizing total proceeds when buyers and sellers disagree about future growth prospects. Earn-outs allow sellers to receive additional payments if the business achieves specific performance targets after the sale, enabling both parties to benefit from exceptional post-sale performance.

Earn-out agreements work best when performance metrics are clearly defined, easily measured, and within the control of the acquiring party. Revenue-based earn-outs are generally preferable to profit-based structures because revenue is harder to manipulate through accounting decisions. Reasonable timeline expectations—typically two to three years maximum—ensure that earn-out periods don't extend indefinitely.

Tax Optimization Strategies

Strategic exit planning requires sophisticated tax optimization that goes far beyond simple capital gains management. The charitable remainder trust structure provides immediate tax deductions while avoiding capital gains taxes and maintaining lifetime income streams from sale proceeds.

Charitable remainder trusts work by transferring business interests to the trust before sale, allowing the trust to sell the business without incurring capital gains taxes. The trust then pays annual income to the original business owner for life or a specified term, while the remainder ultimately benefits a chosen charity. This structure provides immediate tax deductions, eliminates capital gains taxes, and creates lifetime income streams while supporting charitable causes.

Opportunity Zone investments offer another sophisticated tax optimization strategy that can defer and potentially eliminate capital gains taxes from business sales. By investing sale proceeds in Qualified Opportunity Zone Funds within 180 days of the sale, business owners can defer capital gains taxes while potentially eliminating taxes on the appreciation of their Opportunity Zone investments.

The key to Opportunity Zone success lies in selecting high-quality investments that can be held for the full ten-year period required to eliminate taxes on appreciation. This strategy works best for business owners who don't need immediate access to their full sale proceeds and can afford to tie up capital in Opportunity Zone investments for a decade.

Strategic Buyer Identification and Negotiation

Strategic buyers often provide the highest valuations because they can capture synergies that financial buyers cannot achieve. Identifying and cultivating relationships with potential strategic buyers becomes a crucial component of exit planning that begins years before you're ready to sell.

Industry consolidators represent one category of strategic buyers who acquire competitors to increase market share and achieve economies of scale. These buyers often pay premium valuations to eliminate competition and gain access to customer relationships that would be expensive to develop organically.

Vertical integrators offer another strategic buyer category that acquires businesses up or down their supply chain to improve margins or control key inputs. Manufacturers might acquire key suppliers to ensure reliable material sources, while distributors might acquire manufacturers to capture additional profit margins.

Technology acquirers focus on businesses that possess valuable intellectual property, customer data, or operational capabilities that complement their existing operations. These buyers often pay significant premiums for businesses that provide technological capabilities they cannot easily develop internally.

Geographic expanders represent strategic buyers who want to enter new markets through acquisition rather than organic expansion. These buyers value existing customer relationships, local market knowledge, and established operations that provide immediate market access without the time and risk associated with starting from scratch.

Negotiation Strategies for Maximum Value

The competitive auction approach creates the highest valuations by generating competition among multiple potential buyers. This strategy requires identifying five to eight potential buyers across different strategic categories, then running simultaneous sales processes that create competitive tension and drive up final valuations.

Successful competitive auctions require comprehensive preparation including detailed business information packages, realistic valuation expectations, and clear timelines that allow all potential buyers to complete their evaluation processes. The goal is creating legitimate competition rather than the appearance of competition, which sophisticated buyers can easily identify and discount.

The relationship-first strategy takes a longer-term approach by building relationships with potential buyers years before you're ready to sell. This approach involves providing value through industry insights, partnership opportunities, or strategic advice that positions you as an obvious acquisition target when buyers are ready to expand through acquisition.

Relationship-based sales often achieve higher valuations because buyers have greater confidence in the business, the management team, and the cultural fit between organizations. These transactions also tend to close more reliably because much of the due diligence has occurred through the relationship-building process.

Exit Timing Optimization

Market window analysis helps identify optimal exit periods by understanding the cyclical patterns that affect business valuations. Quarterly business cycles create seasonal variations in buyer activity, with fourth-quarter exits often benefiting from annual planning and budget cycles, while first-quarter exits take advantage of fresh capital deployment strategies.

Annual market patterns provide additional timing insights, with election years typically seeing reduced merger and acquisition activity due to uncertainty about policy changes. Economic expansion periods generally support higher multiples and more aggressive buyer behavior, while market corrections create opportunities to acquire distressed assets but make selling more challenging.

Business performance timing requires coordinating exit processes with periods of strongest operational performance. Selling during quarters of accelerating growth, expanding margins, or major strategic wins maximizes the impression of business momentum and justifies premium valuations.

The optimal exit timing balances multiple factors including business performance trends, market conditions, personal readiness for transition, and tax optimization opportunities. The most successful exits occur when all these factors align to create maximum value for business owners.

Due Diligence Preparation

Comprehensive due diligence preparation begins months before formal exit processes start. Financial optimization requires working with qualified accountants to ensure financial statements present the strongest possible business performance while maintaining complete accuracy and transparency.

Operational excellence preparation involves documenting business processes to demonstrate systematic operations that don't depend on key individuals. Resolving customer concentration issues, strengthening management teams, and improving operational metrics all contribute to buyer confidence and premium valuations.

Strategic positioning preparation includes developing growth strategies that buyers can implement, identifying acquisition targets that could create additional value, and building competitive analyses that demonstrate market position strength. These materials help buyers envision the future potential of your business under their ownership.

The most successful due diligence processes anticipate buyer concerns and address them proactively rather than reactively. This preparation demonstrates professionalism and thoroughness that builds buyer confidence while preventing issues that could derail transactions or reduce valuations.

Advanced Exit Structures for Maximum Value

Management buyout options provide control over exit timing while preserving company culture and employee relationships. These structures work well when key managers have the capability and desire to acquire the business, and when owner financing or external capital sources can support the transaction.

Management buyouts often achieve favorable tax treatment while allowing former owners to maintain advisory relationships and potential equity participation in future growth. The success of these transactions depends on realistic valuation expectations and thorough evaluation of management team capabilities.

Private equity partnerships offer growth capital plus future exit optionality by selling majority stakes to private equity firms while retaining significant equity positions. These structures provide immediate liquidity while maintaining upside participation in future value creation.

Private equity partnerships work best when businesses have clear growth opportunities that can benefit from additional capital and operational expertise. The most successful partnerships align incentives between business owners and private equity firms while maintaining operational control during the partnership period.

Risk Management During Exit Processes

Business continuity risks require careful management throughout exit processes to maintain operational performance and customer relationships. Communication strategies must balance transparency with confidentiality, ensuring that key stakeholders understand the process without creating unnecessary uncertainty.

Employee retention becomes critical during exit processes because key personnel departures can derail transactions or reduce valuations. Retention incentives, clear communication about post-sale opportunities, and involvement in transition planning help maintain team stability throughout sale processes.

Deal completion risks include financing contingencies, regulatory approvals, and material adverse change provisions that could prevent transaction completion. Understanding these risks and negotiating appropriate protections ensures that exit processes conclude successfully without unexpected complications.

Post-Exit Wealth Management

Successful exit completion marks the beginning of a new phase in wealth management that requires different strategies and considerations. Immediate priorities include tax payment planning, investment diversification, and lifestyle adjustments that reflect changed income and time allocation patterns.

Long-term wealth preservation requires engaging qualified wealth management professionals who understand the unique challenges and opportunities that come with liquidity events. Investment strategies must balance wealth preservation with growth objectives while maintaining appropriate risk management and diversification.

The most successful post-exit wealth management creates systems for continued wealth building through new investment opportunities, strategic reinvestment, and legacy planning that ensures wealth transfers effectively to future generations.

Your strategic exit represents the culmination of years of systematic business building and empire scaling. By executing a well-planned exit at optimal market timing, you're securing the capital needed for your next wealth-building cycle while demonstrating the discipline that separates professional wealth builders from accidental business owners.

The knowledge and experience gained through building, scaling, and exiting businesses create the foundation for even greater wealth-building opportunities. With substantial capital and proven business acumen, you're positioned to pursue larger opportunities, more sophisticated strategies, and ultimately build the generational wealth that provides true financial freedom for your family.

Your Unbreakable Wealth Legacy

The intelligence explosion has already begun reshaping fortunes across the globe.

You've reached the end of this journey, but in many ways, you're standing at the beginning of something extraordinary. The FIRE Framework isn't just another investment strategy—it's your blueprint for financial independence in an age where artificial intelligence will determine who thrives and who gets left behind. The next several years will separate those who act from those who hesitate, and you now possess the tools to ensure you're among the winners.

This goes beyond money; it's about securing your legacy in a world that's changing faster than most people can comprehend.

The FIRE Framework Revolution You've Learned

You've learned to **Focus** with surgical precision, identifying market dips through technical analysis that separates genuine opportunity from market noise. The divergence patterns between price lows and indicators like CCI and RSI are now part of your investment vocabulary. You understand that economic indicators confirm your technical signals, giving you the confidence to enter markets when others panic.

The **Invest** phase taught you to deploy leveraged instruments with calculated risk management. Index futures, options strategies, and leveraged ETFs are no longer mysterious financial products—they're your tools for capturing AI-driven market surges while protecting your downside. You've learned to calculate position sizing and risk-reward ratios that allow you to sleep well at night while your investments work around the clock.

Reinvest showed you how to transform market profits into tangible business assets. You can now evaluate businesses for their scalability, their resilience to AI disruption, and their potential to generate consistent cash flows. The metrics that matter—unit economics, customer acquisition costs, lifetime value—are now second nature to you.

Finally, **Endure** equipped you with the knowledge to build diversified business portfolios that generate wealth long after the initial AI boom settles. You understand how to acquire businesses that remain essential even as AI dominates their industries, creating multiple income streams that protect your financial future.

The Market Timing Skills You've Developed

Remember when market timing seemed like guesswork? Those days are behind you. You've learned to read the intelligence explosion signals that matter—adoption metrics, sector momentum, and the critical indicators that separate genuine AI advancement from marketing hype. You understand that the 2-3 year window for maximum wealth extraction isn't just a timeline; it's your competitive advantage.

The bubble psychology principles you've mastered will serve you throughout your investing career. You can now distinguish between healthy market corrections and dangerous reversals, understanding that technology explosions follow predictable patterns. This knowledge transforms market volatility from a source of anxiety into a wealth-building opportunity.

Your technical analysis skills have evolved from basic chart reading to sophisticated pattern recognition. You can spot the divergence patterns that signal optimal entry points, and you understand how to combine multiple indicators for confirmation. This isn't about perfect timing—it's about consistently identifying high-probability opportunities that compound over time.

The Business Acquisition Knowledge You've Gained

The transformation from market trader to business owner represents the most significant shift in your wealth-building journey. You've learned to evaluate businesses not just for their current performance, but for their potential to thrive in an AI-dominated economy. The financial metrics that once seemed complex—gross margins, customer concentration, working capital requirements—now inform your acquisition decisions with clarity.

You understand that buying revenue through business acquisition isn't just about cash flow; it's about acquiring assets that appreciate while generating income. The businesses you target have scalable models, defendable market positions, and the flexibility to adapt as AI reshapes their industries.

Your due diligence process has become systematic and thorough. You know how to assess management teams, evaluate competitive moats, and identify the operational improvements that can unlock additional value. This isn't about buying businesses and hoping they perform; it's about acquiring assets you can actively improve.

The Wealth Preservation Foundation You've Built

Wealth creation is only half the equation; wealth preservation completes it. You've learned to establish legal structures that protect your assets from future economic disruption and regulatory changes. The trusts, LLCs, and other entities you've studied aren't just tax optimization tools—they're your insurance policy against uncertainty.

Your understanding of intergenerational wealth transfer ensures that your financial success extends beyond your own lifetime. You've learned to structure your wealth in ways that provide for your family while maintaining control and flexibility. This long-term perspective separates truly wealthy individuals from those who simply have high incomes.

The tax optimization strategies you've discovered can save you hundreds of thousands of dollars over your investing career. But more importantly, you understand that tax planning isn't about avoiding obligations—it's about structuring your wealth to maximize your impact and legacy.

The Risk Management Philosophy You've Embraced

Perhaps the most valuable lesson you've learned is that wealth building during the intelligence explosion isn't about taking bigger risks—it's about taking smarter risks. The defined-risk strategies you've mastered allow you to participate in AI-driven growth while protecting your downside. You understand that leverage amplifies both gains and losses, and you've learned to use it judiciously.

Your position sizing methodology ensures that no single investment can derail your overall strategy. You've learned to think in terms of risk-adjusted returns rather than absolute returns, understanding that consistent gains compound more effectively than sporadic windfalls followed by devastating losses.

The emotional discipline you've developed might be your greatest asset. You understand that market volatility is normal, that corrections are opportunities, and that sticking to your system during difficult periods separates successful investors from the crowd. This psychological edge compounds your technical knowledge.

The Portfolio Management System You've Designed

Your approach to managing multiple businesses and investments has evolved from reactive to proactive. You understand the key performance indicators that matter for each type of asset, and you've learned to implement systems that provide visibility without overwhelming complexity. This operational efficiency allows you to scale your wealth without proportionally increasing your workload.

The diversification principles you've learned extend beyond traditional asset allocation. You understand how to balance growth and income, how to hedge against different types of risks, and how to structure your portfolio for both current cash flow and future appreciation. This holistic approach ensures that your wealth grows in all market conditions.

Your exit planning strategies give you flexibility and options. You understand when to hold, when to sell, and how to structure exits for maximum after-tax proceeds. This forward-thinking approach ensures that you can adapt to changing market conditions while maintaining your wealth-building momentum.

The Intelligence Explosion Advantage You've Secured

The intelligence explosion represents the greatest wealth-building opportunity of your lifetime, and you're positioned to capitalize on it. While others debate whether AI is hype or reality, you're already profiting from the technological shifts that are reshaping entire industries. Your understanding of AI adoption patterns gives you a crucial head start in identifying the businesses and markets that will benefit most from artificial intelligence.

You've learned to view AI not as a threat to existing business models, but as an accelerant for the right types of companies. The businesses you target will use AI to improve their operations, reduce their costs, and expand their market reach. By aligning your investments with these trends, you're positioning yourself to benefit from the productivity gains that AI will generate.

The network effects you've learned to identify become more powerful as AI adoption accelerates. The companies that establish dominant positions in AI-enhanced markets will enjoy increasing returns to scale, creating the type of exponential growth that builds generational wealth. Your framework for identifying these opportunities gives you a significant advantage over investors who are still trying to understand the basics of artificial intelligence.

The Wealth-Building Momentum You've Created

The FIRE Framework isn't just about making money during the intelligence explosion—it's about creating sustainable wealth-building momentum that continues long after the initial AI boom. The technical analysis skills you've developed will serve you throughout your investing career, regardless of market conditions. The business evaluation criteria you've learned will help you identify opportunities in any industry or economic environment.

Your risk management discipline becomes more valuable as your wealth grows. The percentage-based position sizing you've learned scales with your capital, ensuring that your risk controls grow stronger as your portfolio expands. This systematic approach to risk management allows you to take larger positions as your wealth increases without proportionally increasing your risk of catastrophic loss.

The business acquisition skills you've developed become more powerful as you gain experience and credibility. Successful acquisitions provide you with the track record and financial resources to pursue larger opportunities. This creates a virtuous cycle where each successful investment increases your capacity for the next one.

The Legacy Impact You're Building

Your wealth-building journey extends far beyond personal financial gain. The businesses you acquire and improve create jobs, serve customers, and contribute to economic growth. The systematic approach you've learned can be taught to others, multiplying your impact beyond your direct investments. This creates a legacy that extends beyond financial metrics.

The AI-resilient businesses you're building will provide stability and employment in an economy that's being reshaped by artificial intelligence. By focusing on companies that complement rather than compete with AI, you're contributing to a smoother transition for workers and communities. This alignment between profit and social benefit creates sustainable competitive advantages.

Your understanding of wealth preservation and transfer ensures that your financial success will benefit future generations. The structures you've established will provide your family with both financial security and the knowledge to continue building wealth responsibly. This intergenerational perspective creates lasting impact that extends far beyond your own lifetime.

The Execution Mindset You've Developed

Knowledge without action remains theoretical. The frameworks you've learned become powerful only through consistent application. You understand that successful investing requires both analytical rigor and emotional discipline. The combination of technical knowledge and psychological strength you've developed will serve you throughout your wealth-building journey.

Your systematic approach to decision-making reduces the influence of emotions and biases that derail most investors. You've learned to trust your analysis, stick to your plan, and maintain perspective during both bull and bear markets. This disciplined approach compounds your technical advantages.

The continuous learning mindset you've embraced ensures that your skills will evolve with changing market conditions. You understand that the principles remain constant, but the specific applications adapt to new opportunities and challenges. This flexibility allows you to maintain your edge as markets and technologies continue to evolve.

The Transformation You're About to Achieve

You began this journey facing uncertainty about AI's impact on your financial future. You worried about missing opportunities, making costly mistakes, or becoming irrelevant in a rapidly changing economy. Those concerns have been replaced by confidence in your ability to identify, evaluate, and capitalize on AI-driven opportunities.

The FIRE Framework has transformed your relationship with market volatility. Instead of fearing corrections and uncertainty, you now view them as wealth-building opportunities. This mindset shift alone will generate significant returns over your investing career, as you'll be buying when others are selling and remaining calm when others panic.

Your evolution from concerned observer to confident actor in the intelligence explosion represents a fundamental shift in your financial trajectory. You're no longer reacting to market events—you're anticipating them and positioning yourself to benefit from them. This proactive approach compounds your returns and reduces your stress.

The Future You're Shaping

The next few years will validate your decision to embrace the FIRE Framework. As AI adoption accelerates and reshapes entire industries, you'll be positioned to capture the gains that this technological revolution generates. Your systematic approach to market timing, business acquisition, and wealth preservation will create multiple income streams that provide both growth and security.

The businesses you acquire will benefit from AI-driven productivity improvements, giving you exposure to the technology's upside without the risks associated with speculative investments. Your diversified portfolio will generate cash flow that funds additional opportunities, creating a compound effect that accelerates your wealth building.

Your preserved and protected wealth will provide security for your family and funding for your philanthropic goals. The legal structures you've established will ensure that your success creates lasting benefits that extend beyond your own lifetime. This creates a legacy that combines financial success with meaningful impact.

The intelligence explosion belongs to those who extract gains to build moats, and you now possess the tools to do exactly that. Your unbreakable wealth legacy starts with the next decision you make, the next opportunity you evaluate, and the next step you take toward implementing everything you've learned.

The window is open, the tools are in your hands, and your future is waiting to be built.

Glossary

Options Trading Terminology

Understanding options terminology enables you to implement the defined-risk strategies essential to the Invest step of the FIRE Framework. These terms form the foundation of your leveraged market approach.

Call Option: A contract giving you the right to buy 100 shares of stock at a specific price within a certain time period. You pay a premium for this right but aren't obligated to exercise it.

Put Option: A contract giving you the right to sell 100 shares of stock at a specific price within a certain time period. Useful for protecting positions or betting on price declines.

Strike Price: The predetermined price at which you can buy (call) or sell (put) the underlying stock. Choose strikes based on your risk tolerance and profit objectives.

Expiration Date: The last day you can exercise your option. Options lose value as they approach expiration, making timing crucial for profitability.

Premium: The price you pay to purchase an option. This represents your maximum risk for buying options and your immediate income for selling options.

Intrinsic Value: The actual value of an option if exercised immediately. Calculated as the difference between stock price and strike price for in-the-money options.

Time Value: The portion of an option's premium beyond intrinsic value. This value decreases as expiration approaches, creating opportunities for option sellers.

Implied Volatility: The market's expectation of future price movement. Higher volatility increases option premiums, while lower volatility decreases them.

Delta: Measures how much an option's price changes for each $1 move in the underlying stock. Helps predict option profitability based on stock movement.

Theta: Measures how much an option loses value each day due to time decay. Critical for timing option purchases and sales.

Gamma: Measures how much delta changes as the stock price moves. Higher gamma means delta changes more rapidly with stock price movements.

Vega: Measures how much an option's price changes with volatility changes. Important during earnings announcements and market uncertainty.

Futures Trading Concepts

Futures contracts provide leveraged exposure to market indices, enabling you to capture broad market movements with defined risk parameters.

Contract Size: The standardized amount of the underlying asset represented by one futures contract. E&P 500 futures represent $50 times the index value.

Margin Requirements: The minimum amount of capital required to open and maintain a futures position. Typically 5-10% of contract value.

Initial Margin: The deposit required to open a futures position. This amount varies based on volatility and exchange requirements.

Maintenance Margin: The minimum account balance required to keep a futures position open. Falling below this level triggers a margin call.

Mark-to-Market: The daily settlement process where profits and losses are credited or debited to your account based on closing prices.

Leverage Ratio: The relationship between contract value and margin required. Higher leverage amplifies both profits and losses.

Rollover: The process of closing an expiring futures contract and opening a new one in a later expiration month.

Contango: A market condition where futures prices are higher than current spot prices, typically indicating an upward-sloping yield curve.

Backwardation: A market condition where futures prices are lower than current spot prices, often seen in commodity markets.

Business Valuation Methods

Accurate business valuation ensures you pay appropriate prices for acquisitions while identifying undervalued opportunities.

Multiple-Based Valuation: Using industry-standard multiples to estimate business value based on revenue, EBITDA, or other financial metrics.

Discounted Cash Flow (DCF): Projecting future cash flows and discounting them to present value using an appropriate discount rate.

Asset-Based Valuation: Calculating business value based on tangible and intangible assets minus liabilities.

Comparable Sales: Analyzing recent sales of similar businesses to establish market-based valuation ranges.

Earnings Multiple: The ratio of purchase price to annual earnings, typically ranging from 3-7 times for small businesses.

Revenue Multiple: The ratio of purchase price to annual revenue, useful for businesses with irregular earnings patterns.

EBITDA Multiple: The ratio of purchase price to earnings before interest, taxes, depreciation, and amortization.

Market Risk Indicators

Understanding market risk helps you implement appropriate position sizing and risk management protocols.

Beta: Measures a stock's or portfolio's sensitivity to market movements. Beta of 1.0 moves with the market, while higher betas amplify market movements.

Standard Deviation: Measures the volatility of returns around the average return. Higher standard deviation indicates greater risk.

Sharpe Ratio: Measures risk-adjusted returns by comparing excess return to standard deviation. Higher ratios indicate better risk-adjusted performance.

Maximum Drawdown: The largest percentage decline from peak to trough in portfolio value. Helps assess worst-case scenario risk.

Value at Risk (VaR): Estimates the maximum expected loss over a specific time period at a given confidence level.

Correlation: Measures how closely two investments move together. Low correlation provides diversification benefits.

Alpha: Measures investment performance relative to a benchmark. Positive alpha indicates outperformance after adjusting for risk.

AI and Technology Terms

Specialized terminology for evaluating AI-era investment opportunities and understanding technology-driven market dynamics.

Artificial Intelligence (AI): Computer systems performing tasks typically requiring human intelligence, including learning, reasoning, and problem-solving.

Machine Learning: A subset of AI where systems automatically improve performance through experience without explicit programming.

Deep Learning: Advanced machine learning using neural networks with multiple layers to analyze complex patterns in data.

Natural Language Processing (NLP): AI technology enabling computers to understand, interpret, and generate human language.

Computer Vision: AI technology enabling machines to interpret and analyze visual information from images or videos.

Cloud Computing: Delivery of computing services over the internet, providing scalable resources without physical infrastructure.

Software as a Service (SaaS): Software delivery model where applications are hosted centrally and accessed via subscription.

API (Application Programming Interface): Software intermediary allowing different applications to communicate and share data.

Data Analytics: The process of examining datasets to draw conclusions and inform business decisions.

Automation: Technology performing tasks with minimal human intervention, increasing efficiency and reducing costs.

Digital Transformation: Integration of digital technology into business operations, changing how companies operate and deliver value.

Blockchain: Distributed ledger technology providing secure, transparent transaction recording without central authority.

Cryptocurrency: Digital currencies secured by cryptography and operating on decentralized networks.

Fintech: Financial technology companies using software to provide financial services more efficiently than traditional institutions.

Cybersecurity: Protection of digital systems, networks, and data from digital attacks and unauthorized access.

References

Avoid wash sale for tax purposes: Stock trading tips 2025. (n.d.). *Investment Guide.* https://investmentguide.co.uk/what-is-a-wash-sale-and-how-to-avoid-it-for-tax-purposes-when-buying-and-selling-stocks/

Benzinga. (2025, May 15). Jeff Bezos once watched Amazon's stock collapse from $113 to $6 but held on to the belief that the stock is not the company. Here's how he weathered that. *Benzinga.* https://www.benzinga.com/tech/25/05/45426247/jeff-bezos-once-watched-amazons-stock-collapse-from-113-to-6-but-held-on-to-the-belief-that-the-stock-is-not-the-company-heres-how-he-weathered-that-st

Bhootra, A. (2024). Predicting returns using moving averages: The role of investor inattention. *Managerial Finance, 50*(6), 1066–1088. https://doi.org/10.1108/MF-04-2023-0257

Calculate and cut the customer acquisition cost (CAC). (n.d.). *Pipedrive.* https://www.pipedrive.com/en/blog/customer-acquisition-cost

Charles Schwab. (n.d.). The Greeks: Trading with an edge. *Schwab Learning Center.* Retrieved July 23, 2025, from https://www.schwab.com/learn/story/understanding-options-greeks

Essential steps to automate your business processes. (n.d.). *The Core Soft.* https://thecoresoft.com/essential-steps-to-automate-your-business-processes.html

Fidelity Investments. (n.d.). Options trading: What are options? Retrieved July 23, 2025, from https://www.fidelity.com/learning-center/investment-products/options/options

Finding the proper stock entry. (n.d.). *Eat, Sleep, Trade.* https://www.eatsleeptrade.net/finding-the-proper-stock-entry

Fit Small Business. (2024, July 4). Best SBA funded & highest SBA default rate franchises. *Fit Small Business.* https://fitsmallbusiness.com/best-franchises-sba-default-rates/

Franchise Budget Blinds. (2023, October 31). Franchise success rates: 2023 franchise statistics. *Budget Blinds*. https://franchise.budgetblinds.com/blog/franchise-success-rates-2023-franchise-statistics/

From sole proprietor to LLC: Unlocking growth and protecting your business. (n.d.). *Weston Tax Associates*. https://www.westontax.com/from-sole-proprietor-to-llc-unlocking-growth-and-protecting-your-business/

Gluu. (n.d.). Lean process improvement: Removing the waste. *Gluu*. https://gluu.biz/lean-process-improvement/

Kraken. (2025, May 28). How to keep your crypto safe. *Kraken*. https://www.kraken.com/learn/how-keep-crypto-safe

LendingTree. (2025, April 7). Percentage of businesses that fail — And how to boost chances of success. *LendingTree*. https://www.lendingtree.com/business/small/failure-rate/

Live Oak Bank. (n.d.). How much is the down payment for a business acquisition loan? Retrieved July 24, 2025, from https://www.liveoakbank.com/article/how-much-down-payment-business-acquisition-loan/

Meadows, D. H. (2008). *Thinking in systems*. Florida Tech Research Labs and Institutes. https://research.fit.edu/media/site-specific/researchfitedu/coast-climate-adaptation-library/climate-communications/psychology-amp-behavior/Meadows-2008.-Thinking-in-Systems.pdf

Network effects (The hidden engine behind billion-dollar empires). (n.d.). *10 Minute MBA*. https://newsletter.10minmba.com/p/network-effects-the-hidden-engine

Passive Secrets. (2025, March 18). 80+ interesting franchise statistics & facts (2025 report). *Passive Secrets*. https://passivesecrets.com/franchise-statistics/

Principal investment: Its definition, and purpose. (n.d.). *Tycoonstory*. https://www.tycoonstory.com/principal-investment-its-definition-purpose-and-operational-process/

Rodrigue, J.-P. (2008). Stages in a bubble. *Hofstra University*. https://people.hofstra.edu/jean-paul_rodrigue/jpchartstheconomics/stages_bubble.html

Scott, M. (2024, February 21). Maximizing tax efficiency in legacy planning: Strategies for generational wealth. *LinkedIn*. https://www.linkedin.com/pulse/maximizing-tax-efficiency-legacy-planning-strategies-scott-mba-ea-q2lcc

Stop losing money: 12 common trading mistakes to fix. (n.d.). *Big Brain Money*. https://bigbrainmoney.com/12-common-trading-mistakes-to-avoid/

The future of entrepreneurship in a world where AI is dominating. (n.d.). *Due*. https://due.com

The ultimate guide to creative tax deductions for small businesses in 2024. (n.d.). *Ledgerment*. https://ledgerment.com/resources/creative-tax-deductions-for-small-business/

Understanding emotions during the four market stages. (n.d.). *The Technical Traders*. https://thetechnicaltraders.com/understanding-emotions-during-the-four-market-stages/

U.S. Small Business Administration. (n.d.). 7(a) loans. https://www.sba.gov/funding-programs/loans/7a-loans

www.ingramcontent.com/pod-product-compliance
Lightning Source LLC
LaVergne TN
LVHW090409210926
848480LV00002B/507